FRESH FLAVORS
for the
SLOW COOKER

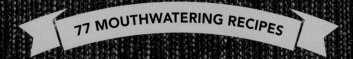

77 MOUTHWATERING RECIPES

Nicki Sizemore

Storey Publishing

The mission of Storey Publishing is to serve our customers by publishing practical information that encourages personal independence in harmony with the environment.

EDITED BY Deanna F. Cook and Sarah Guare
ART DIRECTION AND BOOK DESIGN BY Ash Austin
TEXT PRODUCTION BY Jennifer Jepson Smith
INDEXED BY Christine R. Lindemer, Boston Road Communications

COVER AND INTERIOR PHOTOGRAPHY BY © Philip Ficks
ADDITIONAL PHOTOGRAPHS BY © Floortje/iStock.com, 41; © joebelanger/iStock.com, 17; Mars Vilaubi: iii, 19, 59, 97, 139, 171
FOOD STYLING BY Tehra Thorp

Storey books are available at special discounts when purchased in bulk for premiums and sales promotions as well as for fund-raising or educational use. Special editions or book excerpts can also be created to specification. For details, please call 800-827-8673, or send an email to sales@storey.com.

Storey Publishing
210 MASS MoCA Way
North Adams, MA 01247
storey.com

Printed in China through Asia Pacific Offset
10 9 8 7 6 5 4 3 2 1

Library of Congress Cataloging-in-Publication Data

Names: Sizemore, Nicki, author.
Title: Fresh flavors for the slow cooker / Nicki Sizemore.
Description: North Adams : Storey Publishing, 2019. | Includes index. | Summary: "Fresh Flavors for the Slow Cooker is filled with slow-simmered main dishes, plus 35 recipes for sauces and sides, that replace canned ingredients with fresh vegetables, boost flavor with aromatic herbs and spices, and feature a tantalizing array of global tastes in dishes that span the menu. Whether you're feeding a family or entertaining a crowd, each recipe highlights prep work that can be knocked out days in advance, making serving meals worthy of every occasion easy and delicious"— Provided by publisher.
Identifiers: LCCN 2019023390 (print) | LCCN 2019023391 (ebook) | ISBN 9781635861235 (paperback) | ISBN 9781635861242 (ebook)
Subjects: LCSH: Electric cooking, Slow. | LCGFT: Cookbooks.
Classification: LCC TX827 .S537 2019 (print) | LCC TX827 (ebook) | DDC 641.5/884--dc23
LC record available at https://lccn.loc.gov/2019023390
LC ebook record available at https://lccn.loc.gov/2019023391

For Mom, who convinced me to give my slow cooker another chance

Contents

1 VEGETABLES

2 CHICKEN, TURKEY & PORK

BEEF & LAMB

SEAFOOD

BREAKFAST & BRUNCH

Introduction
Rethink the Old

I confess: I haven't always loved my slow cooker. For years it collected dust on a basement shelf, hauled upstairs only once or twice a year to simmer a batch of chili. While I wanted to like it (what could be better than an appliance that will cook dinner for you?!), the recipes I tried consistently turned out dull or watery or, worst of all, both. After several disappointing meals, starting with a cream-of-something disaster and ending with a tough-as-leather pork loin, I threw in the towel.

To be honest, it wasn't until a couple of years ago that I started to reconsider that dusty lady. With two kids, a dog, busy jobs, and never-ending afternoon and evening activities, I needed backup in the kitchen. While I had been relying on a small handful of kitchen appliances to help me get dinner on the table fast — the food processor for chopping and puréeing, the high-speed blender for quick sauces and smoothies, and the rice cooker for making big batches of whole grains and rice — none could meet the promise of the slow cooker. It could actually *cook* our meals — unattended (!!) — while we went about our days.

I started tinkering with a few slow cooker recipes, ditching the canned goods for fresh ingredients, cutting back on the liquid to prevent the food from turning watery, amping up the aromatics (such as onions and garlic) and spices to inject lots of flavor, and finishing the cooked dishes with quick but vibrant sauces or toppings. Much to my excitement, I discovered that it is possible to create mouthwatering meals in the slow cooker — from succulent meatballs to vegetarian Thai curries and holiday-worthy braises.

Fast-forward to today. I am now *infatuated* with my slow cooker. Sure, she might not be all that technologically flamboyant, but the slow cooker can be utterly indispensable when it comes to getting unbelievably *delicious* dinners on the table on busy weeknights. Even more, it's my secret tool for making stress-free yet elegant meals when entertaining.

Weeknight Warrior

The stress of getting dinner on the table can be exponentially reduced with the help of the slow cooker, not simply because it cooks your food all day but because it takes away the dinnertime stress of figuring out what to make. Whereas I would usually wait until the evening witching hour — when life is at its most stressful in my house — to start cooking dinner, I began to get into the habit of prepping meals in the morning, or at lunch, or best yet, the day before, then letting the slow cooker do its job. Since the mealtime hour was simplified, I was even freed up to make sauces and sides if I felt the urge.

The slow cooker has become a weeknight warrior in my house, regularly helping me knock out not only dinner but also breakfast and brunch. Through a whole bunch of testing (and retesting and retesting!), I developed recipes that pass my strict taste tests while also being accessible enough for any old Tuesday. I use the slow cooker to bake sweet potatoes, which we stuff like giant nachos (page 39); I simmer up all sorts

The slow cooker is an amazing tool to help us transform those fresh ingredients into delectable meals.

of soups, such as a veggie-packed minestrone and creamy Thai Curried Chicken and Rice Noodles; I make ribs and carnitas, which in the past I would cook only on weekends; and I even slow-cook a comforting pumpkin brown rice pudding while we sleep. My family gets wholesome, satisfying, downright *delectable* meals that I feel good about, and I get to avoid some of that mealtime anxiety.

Not Quite a Grandma (but Close)

This might be a good time to dispel a few myths about the slow cooker. As much as we might want to imagine it as a little grandma toiling away in the kitchen all day making us dinner, in reality it's more like a babysitter watching over your kids while you're gone and having them brushed and bathed by the time you get home. While the slow cooker doesn't actually make your dinner, it looks after it with gentle care, transforming the ingredients into something that's much more scrumptious than the sum of its parts (just as my kids are *way* more delicious once they're clean and bathed).

A few decades ago, slow cooker recipes relied on a slew of processed and/or canned ingredients that could be dumped in and abandoned. While those recipes admittedly required very little work, they made up for it in their, let's say, "strange" flavor and texture (do the words *bland* and *mushy* come to mind?). With wider access to fresh foods and spices than ever before, our palates have undoubtedly changed for the better. The slow cooker is an amazing

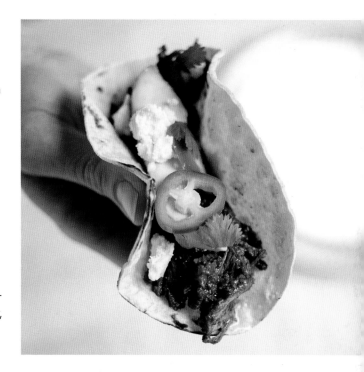

tool to help us transform those fresh ingredients into delectable meals, but it does require a bit of legwork. Just as you would get your kids ready and write out instructions for a babysitter (then give the kids a snuggle once you got home), you'll need to do some prep work before assembling the slow cooker and then finish off the dish before eating.

But here's the thing. Even if you spend time in the morning (or the day before) prepping the ingredients to go into the slow cooker, I promise you this: when you walk through the door hours later and dinner is already simmering away, it will *feel* like there's a little grandma sitting on your countertop doing all the work for you. And let me tell you, it feels freaking great.

My slow cooker has become a weeknight warrior in my house.

Weekend Sous Chef

I don't just use my slow cooker during the work-week — it's also my secret weapon when we have guests over. I love to entertain, but to be honest, I'm a bit of a nervous host as I tend to stress about the details. I realized some time ago that if I can cook most of the meal before my friends arrive, I'm much more relaxed and have way more fun — I can enjoy our company instead of being stuck at the stove all night. The slow cooker is queen when it comes to making meals ahead of time. Many of these recipes even improve with age, meaning you can cook the entree for your Saturday-night dinner party on Thursday, and nobody will be the wiser.

There are plenty of dishes in this book that are perfect for special occasions or parties, such as melt-in-your mouth short ribs with Creamy Parmesan Polenta, which is comfort food at its most elegant; Asian Pork Lettuce Wraps and Bibimbap Beef Bowls, which are interactive and fun to eat; and my favorite Lamb Ragù with Ricotta and Mint, which is heavenly over pappardelle pasta. You can even make an easy bouillabaisse in the slow cooker, which is one of my favorite dinners in early fall, or perfectly poached salmon fillets, which I love to serve out on our back deck once the weather warms.

Other recipes — such as Pulled Pork Sand-wiches, rich Best Beef Chili, and Shredded Beef Mole Tacos — are perfect for less formal occasions, such as football games or potlucks. And let's not forget about brunch! I can throw together a French Toast Casserole or a Spinach, Prosciutto, and Gruyère Strata for leisurely weekend gatherings or holidays, freeing me up to relax with a cup of tea and the paper before my guests arrive (ha, if only — you'll find me frantically straightening up the living room!).

Side dishes transform each of the slow cooker recipes into vibrant, well-rounded meals.

Sauces & Sides (Optional!)

One of my favorite things to do as a chef and educator is create menus, and as a mom I carve out time each week to write up a weeknight dinner plan for my family. However, not everybody shares this passion. (As one of my friends recently put it bluntly, "Menu planning completely sucks.") In this book, I tried to take some of that work off your shoulders. I've included optional accompaniments and/or side dishes to transform each of the slow cooker recipes into vibrant, well-rounded meals. For example, Chipotle Crema adds sweet smokiness to Black Bean Soup, Quick Pickled Red Onions brighten up Carnitas Tacos, and Tzatziki Sauce provides creamy contrast to Lamb Gyros. Likewise, Skillet Cornbread is perfect for dunking into Vegetable and Quinoa Chili, and crunchy Red Cabbage and Sweet Corn Slaw is just right piled on top of (or alongside) the Pulled Pork Sandwiches. But for those nights when homemade cornbread isn't going to happen, serve the chili with tortilla chips instead. Swap in preshredded slaw mix for the red cabbage. Go for plain sour cream, raw red onion, and store-bought tzatziki. You get it. While I adore all the side dish recipes included in these pages (and my kids applaud them, too), there is absolutely nothing wrong with taking shortcuts when you need to — *this is about making nourishing meals that work for you and your family.*

There's one last thing I'd like to say before we jump into the meaty bulk of this book. This is my third cookbook, and while I've loved writing each one, this book has been the most enjoyable. I wasn't stuck testing recipes during the dinnertime rush, since the prep work happened earlier in the day. More important, however, is that even after nine solid months of testing recipes five or six days a week, we never tired of the dishes. In fact, these are some of our very favorite family meals, and I hope they will become some of yours as well.

I would love to hear from you! Please reach out and share your comments, questions, and pictures (I love pictures!) on Instagram at @fromscratchfast.

xo,

Slow Cooker
Tips & Techniques

1. Pick the right size and shape.

The majority of the recipes in this book call for a 4- to 7-quart slow cooker, although some larger-volume dishes and bigger cuts of meat require a larger size (5 to 7 quarts). I've found the sweet spot to be around 6 quarts, which can accommodate nearly any soup or stew recipe and is also big enough to fit large cuts of meat, fish fillets, and whole vegetables. I highly recommend oval-shaped slow cookers (as opposed to round ones), which better fit whole roasts, long fish fillets, casseroles, and braises. In addition, since they have a wider surface area, oval slow cookers tend to cook foods more evenly.

2. Know your model.

Different brands and models of slow cookers vary in their temperature ranges. I include suggested cooking times for both low and high settings (where applicable), but you'll still want to get to know your own slow cooker. If your recipes tend to be done on the early side, you'll know that your model runs a bit hotter, whereas if your dishes are done on the later end, your slow cooker is on the cooler side. From there you can better estimate your cooking times and adjust accordingly.

Slow Cooker vs. Multicooker

A traditional slow cooker is different from a multicooker (such as an Instant Pot). A multicooker is a programmable electric pressure cooker, steamer, yogurt maker, and slow cooker all in one. They're best known for their pressure-cooking function, which allows you to cook hearty foods such as grains, beans, tough cuts of meat, and rice in a fraction of the time that they would take on the stove. Their slow cooker function, however, isn't as reliable and performs differently than traditional slow cookers. Multicookers tend to come to temperature really quickly, meaning they cook delicate foods such as chicken pieces, vegetables, and fish much faster than traditional slow cookers. Conversely, because of the design of their heating element, multicookers are less efficient at slow cooking thick, tough cuts of meat such as bone-in short ribs or pork shoulder — those foods can take considerably longer to cook through. It's also harder to check on the food in a multicooker, as you have to wait for the steam to fully escape before opening the lid.

While I love my multicooker for whipping up quick batches of grains and beans, or for cooking a whole piece of meat or hardy vegetables fast, when it comes to slow cooking, I stick with my traditional slow cooker. Its gentle, consistent heat just can't be matched, and I can confidently leave food unattended for hours.

3. Get a jump start.

Whenever possible, I include "jump-start" tips in the recipes, which are prep steps that can be knocked out the day — or even a couple of days — before, such as chopping vegetables or sautéing onions and garlic. For me, this is key on busy weekdays. I can chop all the veggies for the soup or slather a spice rub on the meat the night before, then toss them in the slow cooker with the remaining ingredients in the morning. Refrigerate chopped vegetables in airtight containers or in ziplock bags, or simply combine the ingredients in the removable insert and pop the whole thing in the fridge. (For ceramic models, be sure to bring the insert back to room temperature before heating, to prevent cracking.) For aromatics that need to be cooked first, such as onions, store them separately or go ahead and sauté (or microwave!) them the day before.

4. Sauté vegetables . . . or not.

Sometimes you need to cook certain aromatics before adding them to the slow cooker. For instance, diced onions have a tendency to overpower a soup or stew and never quite soften completely if they're added raw (I don't know about you, but I can't stand crunchy onions in a soup!). However, the good news is that aromatics need only about 3 minutes in a pan before going into the slow cooker, and *even better*, you can actually cook them in a microwave instead! I include both options in the recipes where needed (not all recipes require precooking), and, trust me, it makes a huge difference in the finished dish. If you have a slow cooker

with a sauté function, you can cook the aromatics right in the slow cooker before adding the rest of the ingredients.

5. Sear meat . . . sometimes.

While many cuts of meat (such as chicken thighs, pork shoulder, and ground turkey) can go straight into the slow cooker without browning, other hearty or fatty cuts (such as short ribs, lamb shanks, and ground beef) benefit from searing on the stove first. This allows you to build depth of flavor through caramelization, drain off excess fat, and give the meat an attractive color once cooked. If your slow cooker has a sauté function, you can sear the meat right in the slow cooker. In some recipes, such as the Sriracha Braised Brisket (page 122), caramelization is achieved through broiling the meat at the end of cooking instead of searing it at the beginning.

Searing Ahead

I'm often asked if it's safe to sear meat ahead of time. The USDA advises never to brown meat and then refrigerate it to finish cooking later. The concern is that any bacteria present might not be completely destroyed and could multiply. However, bacteria generally live on the surface of meat, and a thorough sear on all sides should, in theory, kill them off. I'm not advising you to ignore the USDA guidelines, but as long as the meat is refrigerated immediately then cooked thoroughly the following day, it "should" be safe. This goes for larger cuts only — never ground meat, which should always be cooked through. But again, this is a "take it at your own risk" kind of situation, and I therefore do not include browning meat in the jump-start tips.

6. Cut back on liquid.

You'll notice that many of these recipes include a surprisingly small volume of broth, water, or wine. That's because vegetables and meat release a considerable amount of water while cooking, which doesn't evaporate in the slow cooker as it would in a pan. They thus create their own full-flavored braising juices, reducing the need to add a lot of extra liquid at the beginning. (If you add too much liquid, as I did when I first started using my slow cooker, you end up with dull and watery dishes.)

7. Amp up the seasoning.

The slow cooker mellows out flavors during the long cooking time, so it's important to use plenty of bold spices and aromatics such as onions, garlic, and/or ginger. It's also critical to season well with salt and pepper, as they also become muted during cooking. I don't include quantities for salt and pepper in the recipes since my palate might be different from yours, but don't be afraid to season generously!

8. Add quick-cooking vegetables last.

Hearty vegetables — such as root vegetables, squash, and alliums like onions, garlic, and leeks — can simmer all day, turning succulent and tender, but it's best to add delicate vegetables — such as leafy greens, peas, and green beans — to the slow cooker at the end of cooking. That way they'll retain their bright color and texture, lending vibrancy and texture to the finished dish.

Canned Tomatoes

When it comes to slow cooking, canned tomatoes usually trump fresh. Since they're precooked and skinned, they add bright flavor without watering a dish down like fresh tomatoes can. Plus, since they're canned when ripe, they offer great flavor year-round. Several kinds of canned tomatoes are featured throughout this book, which I've broken down for you below.

Whole peeled. These are peeled tomatoes in a purée or juice. I prefer San Marzano tomatoes, which are a specific variety grown in Italy with a superior flavor and texture.

Diced. Diced tomatoes (also stored in a purée or juice) stay firm during cooking, offering a toothsome bite in the final dish.

Fire roasted. You can now find fire-roasted whole, diced, or even crushed tomatoes, which are cooked over a fire and impart a smoky flavor.

Baby Roma. These are whole baby tomatoes with a sweet, juicy bite (look for Mutti brand). They're a good alternative to diced tomatoes.

Crushed. Crushed tomatoes are milled into a light sauce (sometimes mixed with tomato purée), which is often still a bit coarse.

Strained. Strained tomatoes are usually thicker and smoother than crushed. Pomi brand is my favorite.

Purée. Tomato purée is the thickest and richest of the canned tomatoes (excluding paste), with a deeper flavor.

Paste. This is the most concentrated form of tomato products, made by cooking down tomatoes to a thick paste. I prefer to buy it in tubes, which can be stored in the fridge for months.

9. Ditch the lean cuts.

The slow cooker is queen for rendering meat ultratender and silky, but it can have an adverse affect on lean cuts, turning them dry or chalky. I therefore prefer to stick with richer cuts, such as chicken thighs instead of breasts, pork shoulder instead of loin, and beef chuck instead of tenderloin.

10. Don't be afraid to cook fish.

My biggest revelation when writing this book was to discover that the slow cooker is a fantastic tool for cooking fish! When layered over citrus slices with a touch of liquid such as water and wine, fish fillets steam gently until flaky and moist. Similarly, when chunks of fish and shellfish are added to a stew at the end of cooking, they slowly poach until perfectly cooked through.

11. Keep the lid closed.

While it's tempting to check on that simmering stew, unless it's near the end of the cooking time, it's best to leave the lid closed. The slow cooker builds up heat over time and maintains an even, low temperature. When you open the lid, the steam escapes and the temperature drops, which can reduce the slow cooker's efficacy. So while it's fine to check near the end (or to stir if directed to do so in the recipe), keep that lid on!

12. Use a foil sling for delicate foods.

Lining the slow cooker with foil can be a useful way to cook delicate items (such as fish fillets) or casseroles (such as the strata, page 183) that you want to remove at the end. The foil is used as a sling to remove the entire contents of the slow cooker after cooking. This prevents fragile foods like fish fillets from breaking apart, and it allows you to serve a strata whole for an attractive presentation.

13. Cook ahead.

Many of the dishes in the following pages, including most of the soups, stews, and braised meats, taste even better after a day or two in the fridge (meaning you can cook them ahead of time — a godsend for entertaining). Cool the dishes to room temperature before refrigerating. Store braised meats right in their cooking sauce. If your slow cooker has a removable insert, you can pop the whole insert in the fridge (just be sure to bring it to room temperature before reheating to prevent cracking). Remove any hardened pieces of fat before reheating.

14. Freeze your leftovers.

One of the best features about slow cooker meals is that they store wonderfully, making for awesome leftovers. Most of the dishes in the following pages can be refrigerated for several days or frozen for a few months (it's so nice to have dinner waiting for you in the freezer!). Store leftovers in airtight containers or freezer-safe ziplock bags (squeeze out the excess air if using bags and use snug containers to prevent freezer burn). Also, be sure to mark the containers with the contents and the date so that you don't forget what they are (I always swear I'll remember, then swear when I don't!).

Defrosting and Reheating

Defrost frozen foods in the fridge overnight, or submerge freezer bags in water to defrost foods faster. If any fat has hardened on the surface, remove it before reheating. You can warm the leftovers in the microwave or on the stovetop over gentle heat. If needed, add a few splashes of water to thin.

VEGETABLES

These plant-based recipes are some of our very favorite weeknight meals. The slow cooker makes easy work of simmering up nourishing and nutritious soups, stews, and curries — including Lentil and Veggie Stew with Poached Eggs that tastes far more sumptuous than it would seem, my husband's favorite Thai Vegetable and Peanut Curry, and a superfood Vegetable and Quinoa Chili that my kids adore. We even bake sweet potatoes and make a fuss-free spinach lasagna right in the slow cooker! That's right, Monday; we've got this.

White Bean & Veggie Minestrone + Pesto

PREP TIME: 30 MINUTES
SLOW COOKER TIME: 8–10 HOURS ON LOW

SERVES 6

Whether it's a dreary day that's begging for something nourishing or a sun-filled evening that's calling for a light meal, this vegetable-heavy minestrone always hits the mark. Dried white beans provide substance and don't even need to be soaked before going into the slow cooker — a long, gentle simmer cooks them to perfection. A Parmigiano-Reggiano rind gives the broth a nutty complexity. Zucchini and greens go in near the end to retain their freshness, and cooked pasta is added right before serving, preventing the noodles from turning mushy. A dollop of pesto over each bowl brings the taste of the garden to the table, no matter the season (feel free to use store-bought pesto if basil is not in season).

STOVETOP PREP

- 2 tablespoons extra-virgin olive oil
- 1 medium onion, diced
  Salt and freshly ground black pepper

SLOW COOKER

- 2 quarts vegetable or chicken broth
- 1 (14-ounce) can baby Roma tomatoes (such as Mutti brand) or 1 (14.5-ounce) can diced tomatoes
- 1¼ cups dried cannellini or great northern beans, rinsed and drained
- 3 medium carrots, diced
- 3 large garlic cloves, minced
- 1 (2- to 3-inch) Parmigiano-Reggiano cheese rind
- 1 teaspoon dried Italian seasoning
- ½ teaspoon red pepper flakes
- 3 cups chopped Swiss chard or spinach
- 2 cups diced zucchini (about 2 small zucchini)
  Salt and freshly ground black pepper

PASTA

- ¾ cup macaroni or ditalini pasta (regular or gluten-free)
- 2 tablespoons lemon juice
- 2 tablespoons finely chopped parsley
  Salt and freshly ground black pepper

FOR SERVING

- Pesto (page 23)
- Freshly grated Parmigiano-Reggiano cheese

SLOW COOKER JUMP STARTS
Up to 2 days ahead:
Cook the onion and refrigerate.
Chop and refrigerate the carrots, garlic, Swiss chard, and zucchini (store the zucchini and chard separately).

RECIPE CONTINUES →

PREPARE THE STOVETOP INGREDIENTS

1 Heat the oil in a medium skillet over medium-high heat. Add the onion and season with salt and pepper to taste. Cook, stirring occasionally, until slightly softened, about 3 minutes. (Alternatively, toss the onion with the oil in a heatproof bowl, season with salt and pepper to taste, and microwave on high, stirring occasionally, until softened, 4 to 5 minutes.) Scrape the onion and oil into a 4- to 7-quart slow cooker.

ASSEMBLE THE SLOW COOKER

2 Add the broth, tomatoes, beans, carrots, garlic, Parmigiano-Reggiano rind, Italian seasoning, and pepper flakes to the slow cooker. Cover and cook until the beans are tender, 8 to 10 hours on low (high heat is not recommended, as the beans will fall apart).

3 Add the Swiss chard and zucchini to the slow cooker, and season well with salt and pepper. Cover and cook until the zucchini is bright green and crisp tender, about 20 minutes.

COOK THE PASTA

4 In the meantime, bring a pot of salted water to a boil. Cook the pasta according to the package directions until al dente. Drain.

5 Add the cooked pasta to the soup, along with the lemon juice and parsley. Season well with salt and pepper (the beans soak up a lot of seasoning, so you'll need more than you think).

SERVE

6 Ladle the soup into bowls and dollop with a spoonful of pesto. Sprinkle with grated Parmigiano-Reggiano.

STORAGE
The minestrone can be refrigerated for up to 5 days or frozen for up to 1 month.

Pesto

PREP TIME: 10 MINUTES   **MAKES:** 1 CUP

This classic basil pesto is a staple in our house during summer. Toss it with pasta, dollop it on pizza, spread it on sandwiches and paninis, or spoon it into soups and stews. The pesto can be refrigerated for up to three days — press a piece of plastic wrap directly on its surface to prevent browning.

1 large garlic clove

2 cups lightly packed basil leaves

¼ cup toasted pine nuts

½ cup freshly grated Parmesan or Pecorino Romano cheese, or a mix of both

Juice of ½ small lemon, or more to taste

Salt and freshly ground black pepper

½ cup extra-virgin olive oil

1 Drop the garlic into a food processor with the blade running. Add the basil, pine nuts, cheese, and lemon juice, and season with salt and pepper to taste. Process until finely chopped. Scrape down the sides.

2 With the blade running, slowly pour the oil through the feed tube and process until incorporated.

3 Taste and season with additional salt, pepper, or lemon juice if needed.

Toasting Seeds I prefer to toast seeds like pine nuts, pepitas, and sesame seeds in a large skillet on the stovetop (as opposed to the oven), since they can go from browned to blackened quickly. Spread the seeds in a large pan, and cook them over medium heat, stirring often, until fragrant and lightly browned (pumpkin seeds will start to puff up), 4 to 6 minutes. Toast more than you need, and store leftovers in the fridge or freezer (where they'll keep for months) so that they're ready and waiting to be added to sauces or sprinkled over cooked dishes as a garnish.

Greens & Cheese Lasagna +
Quick Green Salad

PREP TIME: 20 MINUTES
SLOW COOKER TIME: 2–3 HOURS ON LOW

Lasagna used to be a weekend-only affair, before I discovered I could make it in my slow cooker. This simple spinach version is now on our weeknight meal rotation, much to the glee of my two Italian food–loving kids. A quick basil-flecked ricotta mixture gets layered with uncooked lasagna noodles, defrosted frozen spinach or kale, store-bought marinara sauce (I prefer Rao's, which tastes close to homemade), and fresh mozzarella. You'll want to buy mozzarella balls that are wrapped in plastic wrap or that are shrink-wrapped — not the balls in liquid, which could make the lasagna too watery. Also, be sure to buy a good-quality ricotta cheese (nothing with gums or stabilizers). You'll need a 6- to 7-quart oval slow cooker for this recipe. The number of lasagna noodles required will depend on the size of your slow cooker. A quick green salad rounds out the meal.

BASIL RICOTTA
- 1 (15- to 16-ounce) container ricotta cheese (about 2 cups)
- ½ cup freshly grated Parmesan cheese
- 1 large egg
- 1 large garlic clove, finely grated
- 2 tablespoons finely chopped basil
- Pinch of freshly ground nutmeg
- Salt and freshly ground black pepper

SLOW COOKER
- Cooking spray or oil for slow cooker
- 10 ounces frozen chopped spinach or kale, defrosted
- 4 cups marinara sauce (one 32-ounce jar), such as Rao's
- 9–12 lasagna noodles, regular or gluten-free (from one 10- to 12-ounce box)
- 1 pound fresh mozzarella, thinly sliced

FOR SERVING
- Freshly grated Parmesan cheese
- Chopped basil
- Quick Green Salad (page 27; optional)

SLOW COOKER JUMP START
Up to 4 hours ahead:
If you have a removable insert, assemble the lasagna through step 4 (before cooking) and refrigerate.

RECIPE CONTINUES →

MAKE THE BASIL RICOTTA

1 Combine the ricotta, Parmesan, egg, garlic, basil, nutmeg, and salt and pepper to taste in a large bowl.

ASSEMBLE THE SLOW COOKER

2 Spray the inside of a 6- to 7-quart slow cooker with cooking spray, or rub it lightly with oil. Wrap the spinach in a thick layer of paper towels, and squeeze firmly over the sink to remove as much liquid as possible.

3 Spread ½ cup of the sauce over the bottom of the slow cooker. Arrange a layer of the noodles over the top, breaking them to fit and overlapping them as needed (they won't fit in an even layer, and that's fine). Spread half of the basil ricotta over the noodles, followed by half of the spinach and 1 cup of the sauce. Arrange one-third of the mozzarella on top.

4 Repeat the layers, using another layer of noodles, the remaining ricotta, the remaining spinach, and another cup of the sauce. Arrange another layer of mozzarella over the top (reserve the remaining mozzarella in the refrigerator).

5 Place a final layer of noodles over the top, and press down gently to flatten. Spread the remaining sauce evenly on top. Cover and cook on low until the noodles are tender, 2 to 3 hours.

6 Arrange the remaining mozzarella over the top of the lasagna. Wipe off any condensation on the inside of the slow cooker lid, then re-cover and cook until the cheese is melted, about 10 minutes.

SERVE

7 Turn off the slow cooker, pull out the insert (if it is removable), and take off the lid. Let sit for 5 to 10 minutes. Sprinkle the top with grated Parmesan and chopped basil. Serve the lasagna alongside the salad, if desired.

STORAGE
The cooked lasagna can be refrigerated for up to 3 days.

Quick Green Salad

PREP TIME: 5 MINUTES

SERVES: 6

We make this one-bowl green salad almost nightly in my house. A garlic-lemon vinaigrette is whisked together right in the bottom of a salad bowl, and greens are piled on top then tossed before serving. Think of this as a formula rather than a strict recipe. Feel free to sprinkle in nuts, cheese, or chopped vegetables.

½ lemon
1 garlic clove, smashed
1 spoonful Dijon mustard

Salt and freshly ground black pepper
Good-quality extra-virgin olive oil

1 head or bunch of salad greens (the freshest you can find), torn into bite-sized pieces if needed

1 Squeeze the juice from the lemon half into the bottom of a large salad bowl. Add the garlic and rub it around the bowl. If you like a mild dressing, you can pull the clove out, but I'm a garlic lover and always leave it in. Whisk in the mustard and season with salt and pepper to taste. Whisk in oil to taste — you're aiming for about twice as much oil as lemon juice. Dip a lettuce leaf into the dressing and give it a taste. Adjust the flavorings as desired.

2 Pile the lettuce leaves into the bowl. If you're not eating the salad right away, stick the bowl in the fridge without tossing. Right before serving, season the greens with salt and pepper to taste and toss them with the dressing.

Lentil & Veggie Stew
with Poached Eggs

PREP TIME: 20 MINUTES
SLOW COOKER TIME: 7–8 HOURS ON LOW *or* 4–5 HOURS ON HIGH

This stew is one of my favorite meals, no matter what time of year (or time of day — I've been known to eat leftovers for breakfast!). It's richly satisfying but seriously healthy, with loads of vegetables and green lentils. By puréeing some of the stew at the end, you end up with a luxurious, slightly creamy texture that isn't too heavy. While it's delicious as is, a drizzle of pesto lends welcome brightness (feel free to use store-bought pesto if you're pressed for time). An optional poached egg adds a boost of protein and even more opulence. I promise that this is one good-for-you stew that won't leave you hungry. If you're anything like our family, you might want to serve this with chunks of bread for mopping out your bowls.

STOVETOP PREP

1 tablespoon extra-virgin olive oil

1 small onion, finely chopped

SLOW COOKER

5 cups vegetable or chicken broth

1½ cups green lentils, rinsed in cold water

4 medium carrots, finely chopped

2 celery stalks, finely chopped

1 small sweet potato, peeled and finely chopped

4 garlic cloves, minced

3 large thyme sprigs

1 bay leaf
Salt and freshly ground black pepper

1 tablespoon extra-virgin olive oil

2 cups thinly sliced lacinato kale (stems discarded)

½ teaspoon sherry vinegar

FOR SERVING

- Pesto (page 23)
- Poached eggs (see Tip, page 30), optional

SLOW COOKER JUMP STARTS
Up to 2 days ahead:
Cook the onion and refrigerate.
Chop and refrigerate the carrots, celery, sweet potato, and garlic.

RECIPE CONTINUES →

PREPARE THE STOVETOP INGREDIENTS

1 Heat the oil in a medium skillet over medium-high heat. Add the onion and cook, stirring occasionally, until slightly softened, about 3 minutes. (Alternatively, toss the onion with the oil in a heatproof bowl, and microwave on high, stirring occasionally, until softened, 4 to 5 minutes.) Scrape the onion into a 4- to 7-quart slow cooker.

ASSEMBLE THE SLOW COOKER

2 Add the broth, lentils, carrots, celery, sweet potato, garlic, thyme, and bay leaf. Season with salt and pepper to taste and stir to combine. Cover and cook until the vegetables are tender, 7 to 8 hours on low or 4 to 5 hours on high.

3 Remove and discard the thyme sprigs and bay leaf. Transfer 2 cups of the stew to a blender and add the oil. Blend until smooth. Pour the puréed soup back into the slow cooker and stir in the kale. Cover and cook on high until the kale is wilted, about 20 minutes. Stir in the vinegar and season to taste with salt and pepper.

SERVE

4 Ladle the stew into bowls and drizzle with pesto. Top with a poached egg, if using, and sprinkle with a bit more salt and pepper.

STORAGE
The stew can be refrigerated for up to 5 days or frozen for up to 3 months.

How to Poach Eggs With a few simple tricks, poaching eggs is quite simple — I promise! Here's how you do it: Fill a large straight-sided skillet or a wide pot with 3 inches of water. Add ½ teaspoon of white vinegar. Bring the water to a gentle simmer (you should see small, scattered bubbles).

Crack the eggs into individual small bowls or ramekins. Carefully slide one of the eggs into the water, keeping the rim of the bowl right near the surface of the water (this will help the egg keep its shape). If needed, use a spoon to swirl the white around the yolk. Repeat with the other eggs, spacing them at least 1 to 2 inches apart.

Let the eggs cook at a gentle simmer, adjusting the heat as necessary, until the whites are set but the yolks are still jiggly, about 3 minutes. Using a slotted spoon, transfer the eggs to a plate or directly to your soup bowls.

Thai Vegetable & Peanut Curry

PREP TIME: 30 MINUTES
SLOW COOKER TIME: 5–6 HOURS ON LOW *or* 3–4 HOURS ON HIGH

SERVES
6

Whenever we go out for Thai food, my husband, James, orders chicken massaman, a rich coconut-based curry with meat, potatoes, and peanuts. This lighter vegetable-packed curry takes inspiration from that dish, using peanut butter and coconut milk to thicken the sauce. It's now one of James's favorite weeknight meals — and mine, too. Cauliflower and red potatoes give the curry heft, while frozen green beans, which are added at the end, impart brightness and color (you can use 3 cups of baby spinach in place of the green beans, if you prefer). Roasted unsalted peanuts also go right into the curry, providing texture.

STOVETOP PREP

- 1 tablespoon virgin coconut oil
- 1 medium onion, finely chopped
  Salt and freshly ground black pepper
- 3 garlic cloves, minced
- 1 tablespoon minced fresh ginger
- 2 tablespoons red curry paste

SLOW COOKER

- 2 cups low-sodium vegetable or chicken broth
- 1 (14.5-ounce) can diced tomatoes

- 2 tablespoons fish sauce (preferably Red Boat brand)
- 1 tablespoon tamari or soy sauce
- 1 tablespoon packed brown sugar
- 1 large head cauliflower (2½ pounds), cut into 2-inch florets
- 1 pound red potatoes (about 3 medium potatoes), cut into 1-inch pieces
- ½ cup canned coconut milk, well stirred
- ½ cup creamy peanut butter

- 2 cups frozen cut green beans
- ⅓ cup roasted, unsalted peanuts
- 1 tablespoon Sriracha hot sauce
  Salt and freshly ground black pepper

FOR SERVING

- Cooked rice or quinoa
- Coarsely chopped peanuts
- Chopped cilantro
- Sriracha

SLOW COOKER JUMP STARTS
Up to 2 days ahead:
Cook the stovetop ingredients and refrigerate.
Chop the cauliflower and potatoes, and refrigerate separately (store the potato in water to prevent browning, then drain before using).

RECIPE CONTINUES →

PREPARE THE STOVETOP INGREDIENTS

1 Heat the oil in a medium skillet over medium-high heat. Add the onion and season with salt and pepper to taste. Cook, stirring occasionally, until slightly softened, about 3 minutes. Add the garlic, ginger, and curry paste, and cook, stirring, until fragrant, 30 to 60 seconds. Scrape the mixture into a 4- to 7-quart slow cooker. (Alternatively, toss all of the ingredients together in a heatproof bowl, and microwave on high, stirring occasionally, until softened, 4 to 5 minutes.)

ASSEMBLE THE SLOW COOKER

2 Stir in the broth, tomatoes, fish sauce, tamari, and brown sugar. Add the cauliflower and potatoes, and toss to coat. Cover and cook until the vegetables are tender, 5 to 6 hours on low or 3 to 4 hours on high.

3 Combine the coconut milk and peanut butter in a small heatproof bowl, and microwave until warm, about 1 minute (alternatively, you can warm them in a small pot on the stove); stir until smooth. Turn the slow cooker to high (if it's not on high already). Pour the coconut milk mixture into the slow cooker, and add the green beans and peanuts. Cover and cook until warmed through, about 10 minutes. Add the sriracha, and season with salt and pepper.

SERVE

4 Serve the curry over rice or quinoa, and sprinkle with chopped peanuts and cilantro. Drizzle with sriracha.

STORAGE
The curry can be refrigerated for up to 5 days or frozen for up to 3 months.

Squash Curry +
Cilantro, Apple & Cashew Chutney

PREP TIME: 15–20 MINUTES
SLOW COOKER TIME: 6–8 HOURS ON LOW *or* 3–4 HOURS ON HIGH

This is one of the meals I crave most on rainy days and blustery nights. Butternut squash slowly simmers with ginger, garlic, coconut milk, fire-roasted tomatoes, and chickpeas for a slightly sweet curry that's graceful yet comforting, like a ballerina in fleece-lined slippers. I spoon the curry over rice and top it with a cheery Cilantro, Apple, and Cashew Chutney, which is the perfect counterpoint to the warming curry — it's crunchy, tart, sweet, and nutty. Feel free to add a handful or two of spinach to the curry during the last 30 minutes of cooking.

STOVETOP PREP

- 1 tablespoon virgin coconut oil or neutral vegetable oil (such as grapeseed)
- 1 small onion, finely chopped
  Salt and freshly ground black pepper
- 1 tablespoon minced fresh ginger
- 2 garlic cloves, minced
- 1 tablespoon curry powder

SLOW COOKER

- 1 (2½-pound) butternut squash, peeled and cut into 1-inch cubes
- 1 (15-ounce) can chickpeas, drained and rinsed
- 1 (14.5-ounce) can diced fire-roasted tomatoes
- 1 (13.5-ounce) can coconut milk
  Salt and freshly ground black pepper

FOR SERVING

- Cooked rice
- Cilantro, Apple & Cashew Chutney (page 37)
- Naan bread (optional)

SLOW COOKER JUMP STARTS
Up to 3 days ahead:
Cook the stovetop ingredients and refrigerate.
Chop and refrigerate the butternut squash.

RECIPE CONTINUES →

PREPARE THE STOVETOP INGREDIENTS

1 Heat the oil in a medium skillet over medium heat. Add the onion and season with salt and pepper to taste. Cook, stirring occasionally, until softened, about 3 minutes. Add the ginger, garlic, and curry powder. Cook, stirring, until fragrant, 10 to 20 seconds. (Alternatively, combine all of the ingredients in a heatproof bowl, season with salt and pepper, and microwave on high, stirring occasionally, until softened, 4 to 5 minutes.) Scrape the mixture into a 4- to 7-quart slow cooker.

ASSEMBLE THE SLOW COOKER

2 Add the squash, chickpeas, tomatoes, and coconut milk. Season with salt and pepper to taste and stir to combine. Cover and cook until the squash is very tender, 6 to 8 hours on low or 3 to 4 hours on high. Using a fork, mash some of the squash to thicken the curry.

SERVE

3 Serve the curry over cooked rice and sprinkle with the chutney. Serve with naan, if you'd like.

STORAGE
The squash curry can be refrigerated for up to 5 days or frozen for up to 3 months.

Blooming Spices Sautéing (or microwaving) the curry powder with the onion and aromatics before adding it to the slow cooker helps draw out the oils in the spices. This process is called blooming and results in a richer, more rounded flavor.

Cilantro, Apple & Cashew Chutney

PREP TIME: 15 MINUTES   **MAKES:** ABOUT 1 CUP

This crunchy and bright chutney is also delicious sprinkled over soups or tucked into quesadillas.

- 1 tablespoon lime juice
- ½ teaspoon finely grated fresh ginger
- ½ teaspoon honey
- Salt and freshly ground black pepper

- 1 cup lightly packed cilantro leaves and tender stems, finely chopped
- 1 small scallion, finely chopped
- ¼ green apple, finely chopped
- ½ small jalapeño, seeded and finely chopped

- ¼ cup chopped roasted cashews or peanuts
- 1 teaspoon neutral vegetable oil (such as grapeseed)

1 Combine the lime juice, ginger, and honey in a medium bowl and season with salt and pepper to taste. If you have the time, let it sit for 5 minutes to infuse.

2 Add the cilantro, scallion, apple, jalapeño, cashews, and oil. Season with salt and pepper to taste and stir to combine.

TIP

Roasting Nuts I like to roast big batches of nuts — such as cashews, peanuts, almonds, hazelnuts, and pecans — to have on hand as a quick garnish for salads, stir-fries, curries, grain bowls, and more. To toast nuts, spread them on a large baking sheet and bake at 350°F (180°C) for 5 to 10 minutes, until fragrant and slightly darkened (keep an eye on them toward the end of baking, as they can burn quickly). Let cool completely, then store in an airtight container in the fridge or freezer (they'll keep for months).

Fajita Stuffed
Sweet Potatoes + Guacamole

PREP TIME: 15 MINUTES
SLOW COOKER TIME: 6–7 HOURS ON LOW *or* 4–5 HOURS ON HIGH

SERVES
4

Sweet potatoes are a cinch to prepare in the slow cooker, and while they're delicious on their own as a side dish (see the Tip on the next page), in this version the potatoes cook over a bed of chili-spiced peppers and onions. The veggies are tossed with black beans, then are piled over the cooked potatoes, along with cheddar cheese, sour cream, and guacamole. In other words, it's like a healthy-ish version of a fajita or, better yet, a giant nacho! You can thank me later. (P.S. Sometimes I make this specifically to pack for work lunches throughout the week.) You'll need an oval 6- to 7-quart slow cooker for this recipe.

SLOW COOKER

- ½ medium red onion, thinly sliced
- 1 medium green bell pepper, cut into ¼-inch-thick strips
- 1 medium red bell pepper, cut into ¼-inch-thick strips
- 1 medium jalapeño, seeded and finely diced
- 2 large garlic cloves, smashed
- 1 tablespoon chili powder

- 1 teaspoon ground cumin
  Salt and freshly ground black pepper
- 2 tablespoons extra-virgin olive oil
- 4 medium-to-small sweet potatoes (depending on the size of your slow cooker)
- 1 (15-ounce) can black beans, drained and rinsed
- 1 tablespoon chopped cilantro
- 1 teaspoon fresh lime juice

FOR SERVING

- Salt and freshly ground black pepper
- Shredded sharp cheddar cheese
- Sour cream
- Guacamole (page 41)
- Sliced scallions

SLOW COOKER JUMP-START
Up to 1 day ahead:
Chop and refrigerate the onion, peppers, and garlic.

RECIPE CONTINUES →

ASSEMBLE THE SLOW COOKER

1 Scatter the onion, bell peppers, jalapeño, and garlic in the bottom of a 6- to 7-quart oval slow cooker and sprinkle with the chili powder and cumin. Season with salt and pepper to taste, then drizzle with the oil. Toss to combine.

2 Wash and dry the sweet potatoes. Using a small sharp knife, poke each potato in several places, then wrap the potatoes separately in foil. Arrange the potatoes in a single layer on top of the vegetables. Cover and cook until the potatoes are tender when pierced with a knife, 6 to 7 hours on low or 4 to 5 hours on high. Transfer the potatoes to plates.

3 Add the beans, cilantro, and lime juice to the slow cooker, and toss with the vegetables to combine.

SERVE

4 Unwrap the potatoes, discarding the foil. Cut a slit lengthwise in each potato, and squeeze each gently to open. Season the inside of the potatoes with salt and pepper. Spoon the vegetables and beans from the slow cooker over the top of the potatoes. Sprinkle with shredded cheese and top with sour cream and guacamole. Garnish with sliced scallions.

STORAGE
The cooked sweet potatoes and vegetables can be refrigerated for up to 4 days.

Slow Cooker Sweet Potatoes For a fuss-free side dish, you can cook plain sweet potatoes in the slow cooker, and it couldn't be easier! Wash the sweet potatoes but don't dry them (the slight moisture on the skin will help them cook more evenly). Place the potatoes right in the slow cooker (there's no need to wrap them in foil), cover, and cook until the potatoes are tender when pierced with a knife, 6 to 7 hours on low or 4 to 5 hours on high. Serve the sweet potatoes on their own with butter as an easy side dish, or load them up with the toppings of your choice for your entrée — I especially love to smother them with the Best Beef Chili on page 99!

Guacamole

In my opinion, there are few foods as perfect as guacamole. This simple version comes together in no time and makes a big batch, which we pile over our potatoes (or nosh on with tortilla chips). Feel free to cut the recipe in half if you're not so guac obsessed.

2 ripe avocados, pitted
1 small garlic clove, finely grated
Juice from ½ lime, or more to taste

Salt and freshly ground black pepper
1 tablespoon finely chopped cilantro

Scoop the avocado flesh into a small bowl, and add the garlic and lime juice. Mash everything with a fork until creamy but still slightly chunky (or however you like it!). Season with salt and pepper to taste, then fold in the cilantro. Taste and add additional lime juice or cilantro, if desired.

Vegetable & Quinoa Chili +
Skillet Cornbread

PREP TIME: 30 MINUTES
SLOW COOKER TIME: 6–8 HOURS ON LOW *or* 3–5 HOURS ON HIGH

SERVES
6

While I adore the beef chili on page 99, this is the chili that we make most often in our house. It's supremely healthy yet cozy and rich, with a complex but crowd-pleasing flavor. Sweet potato provides a bit of sweetness, while a touch of cacao powder and cinnamon create depth. The chili is thickened with quinoa, which gets cooked right in the slow cooker near the end (it's important to soak the quinoa in water while the chili cooks, which tenderizes the grains so that they cook quickly once added). My kids devour this by the bowlful, especially when topped with an oozy layer of cheddar cheese and big wedges of Skillet Cornbread for dunking (it's also awesome with the jalapeño-cheddar corn muffins on page 101). If you're strapped for time, serve the chili with corn tortilla chips instead.

¼ cup white quinoa

STOVETOP PREP

1 tablespoon extra-virgin olive oil

1 medium onion, diced

SLOW COOKER

1 red, orange, or yellow bell pepper, diced

1 small sweet potato (about 10 ounces), peeled and cut into ½-inch pieces

1 jalapeño, seeded and diced

4 garlic cloves, minced

1 (28-ounce) can diced tomatoes

1 (15-ounce) can pinto beans, drained and rinsed

1 (15-ounce) can great northern beans, drained and rinsed

1 tablespoon chili powder

1 tablespoon raw cacao powder or unsweetened cocoa powder

1 teaspoon ground cumin

1 teaspoon ground coriander

½ teaspoon dried oregano

¼ teaspoon ground cinnamon

1½ cups water

Salt and freshly ground black pepper

FOR SERVING

- Shredded cheddar or Monterey Jack cheese, sour cream, diced avocado, sliced scallions, and/or chopped cilantro, for topping

- Skillet Cornbread (page 45)

SLOW COOKER JUMP STARTS
Up to 2 days ahead:
Cook the onion and refrigerate.
Chop and refrigerate the bell pepper, sweet potato, jalapeño, and garlic.
Measure out the spices.

PREPARE THE QUINOA & STOVETOP INGREDIENTS

1 Place the quinoa in a small bowl and cover with 1 to 2 inches of water. Let sit at room temperature while the chili cooks.

2 Heat the oil in a medium skillet over medium-high heat. Add the onion and cook, stirring occasionally, until slightly softened, about 3 minutes. (Alternatively, toss the onion with the oil in a heatproof bowl, and microwave on high, stirring occasionally, until softened, 4 to 5 minutes.) Scrape the onion into a 4- to 7-quart slow cooker.

ASSEMBLE THE SLOW COOKER

3 Add the bell pepper, sweet potato, jalapeño, garlic, tomatoes, both beans, chili powder, cacao powder, cumin, coriander, oregano, cinnamon, and water, and season well with salt and pepper to taste. Cover and cook until the vegetables are tender, 6 to 8 hours on low or 3 to 5 hours on high. During the last 30 to 40 minutes of cooking, drain the quinoa in a strainer, give it a rinse, and stir it into the chili. Let cook until the quinoa has started to unfurl and the chili has thickened. Taste and season with salt and pepper. Feel free to thin the chili with a few splashes of water if desired (we like it thick!).

SERVE

4 Ladle the chili into bowls and sprinkle with the toppings of your choice. Serve with the cornbread on the side.

STORAGE
The chili can be refrigerated for up to 5 days or frozen for up to 3 months.

Skillet Cornbread

PREP TIME: 15 MINUTES
COOK TIME: 15 MINUTES

SERVES: 8

This is my family's favorite cornbread. It has a slightly sweet crumb and an irresistible golden crust that comes from baking it in a preheated cast-iron skillet. If you don't have buttermilk, check out the hack below. The cornbread can be stored in a covered container at room temperature for up to one day or frozen for up to three months.

1¼ cups cornmeal

1 cup all-purpose or gluten-free flour

3 tablespoons sugar

2 teaspoons baking powder

½ teaspoon baking soda

1 teaspoon fine sea salt

2 large eggs

1½ cups buttermilk

4 tablespoons unsalted butter, melted and cooled slightly

1 tablespoon neutral vegetable oil (such as grapeseed)

1 Preheat the oven to 425°F (220°C). Place a 10-inch cast-iron or ovenproof skillet in the oven for 10 minutes to heat up.

2 In the meantime, whisk together the cornmeal, flour, sugar, baking powder, baking soda, and salt in a large bowl. Make a well in the center of the bowl and crack the eggs into it. Stir the eggs gently to break them up. Add the buttermilk and stir until the wet ingredients are mostly incorporated into the dry ingredients. Pour in the butter and fold until just combined.

3 Take the skillet out of the oven and add the oil. Swirl to coat. Pour the batter into the hot skillet and smooth out the top. Bake for 15 to 18 minutes, until the top is golden brown and a wooden pick inserted in the center comes out clean. Let the bread cool in the skillet on a wire rack for at least 10 minutes before serving.

TIP

Buttermilk Hack No buttermilk? No fear! You can make a hacked version by creating an acidic milk solution. Mix 1½ cups of whole milk with 1½ tablespoons of lemon juice. Let the mixture sit for 5 to 10 minutes, or until it starts to curdle, before using.

Sweet Potato Potage +
Spicy Maple Pecans & Toasted Cheese Baguettes

PREP TIME: 15 MINUTES
SLOW COOKER TIME: 5–6 HOURS ON LOW *or* 3–4 HOURS ON HIGH

I was first introduced to potages (thick, puréed vegetable soups) while studying abroad in the South of France during college. My host *maman* would serve a steaming bowl at the start of every meal during the cold autumn days when the strong, northwesterly mistral winds would blow through the city. The soups became one of my strongest taste memories from my time in France, and I've been making versions of

Maman's potages ever since. This is my family's favorite; it's rich with sweet potatoes, leeks, and a touch of apple, with warming aromas of cinnamon and ancho chile powder. The soup gets drizzled with heavy cream or coconut milk to round out the flavors and is sprinkled with spicy maple pecans for crunch. We love to dunk in thick slices of toasted, cheesy baguettes for a soul-satisfying meal that is *très délicieux* indeed.

SLOW COOKER

2½–3 pounds sweet potatoes (about 2 large potatoes), peeled and cut into 1-inch chunks

1 medium leek, white and light green parts only, halved and cut into ½-inch slices

1 medium carrot, cut into ½-inch rounds

¼ green apple, cored, peeled, and chopped

1 bay leaf

¼ teaspoon ground cinnamon

⅛ teaspoon ancho chile powder or pinch of cayenne pepper

Salt and freshly ground black pepper

3 cups low-sodium vegetable or chicken broth

2 cups water

½ teaspoon lemon juice

FOR SERVING

- Heavy cream or coconut milk
- Spicy Maple Pecans (page 49)
- Toasted Cheese Baguettes (page 50)

SLOW COOKER JUMP STARTS
Up to 1 day ahead:
Chop and refrigerate the sweet potatoes, leek, carrot, and apple.
Combine all of the slow cooker ingredients and refrigerate.

RECIPE CONTINUES →

ASSEMBLE THE SLOW COOKER

1 Place the sweet potatoes, leek, carrot, and apple in a 4- to 7-quart slow cooker. Add the bay leaf, cinnamon, and chile powder. Season well with salt and pepper to taste. Pour in the broth and water, and stir to combine. Cover and cook until the vegetables are very tender, 5 to 6 hours on low or 3 to 4 hours on high.

2 Remove and discard the bay leaf. Purée the soup in a blender or by using a stick blender (if you prefer a thinner consistency, add more water to loosen). Stir in the lemon juice, and season with salt and pepper.

SERVE

3 Ladle the soup into bowls, and drizzle with heavy cream or coconut milk. Crumble some spicy pecans over the top. Serve the soup with cheese baguettes for dunking.

STORAGE
The soup can be refrigerated for up to 5 days or frozen for up to 3 months.

Broth or Water? Store-bought vegetable broths vary widely in flavor, with some being quite strong. When making vegetable soups, I therefore prefer to use a mix of broth and water, ensuring that the fresh taste of the vegetables will shine through.

Spicy Maple Pecans

PREP TIME: 5 MINUTES

COOK TIME: 5–7 MINUTES

MAKES: ¾ CUP

These sweet and spicy nuts are completely irresistible. You can bake them at the same time as the Toasted Cheese Baguettes. They can be refrigerated for up to one month.

¾ cup pecans

2 teaspoons maple syrup

⅛ teaspoon ground cinnamon

⅛ teaspoon cayenne pepper

Salt

1 Preheat the oven (or a toaster oven) to 400°F (200°C). Line a small baking sheet with parchment paper.

2 Pour the pecans onto the baking sheet, and drizzle with the maple syrup. Sprinkle with the cinnamon and cayenne, and season with salt to taste. Toss well to coat, then spread in a single layer. Bake for 5 to 7 minutes or until the nuts are a shade darker in color and aromatic. Sprinkle with a bit more salt, and let cool (the nuts will harden as they cool).

Toasted Cheese Baguettes

PREP TIME: 5 MINUTES
COOK TIME: 10 MINUTES

SERVES: 6

These garlicky toasted cheese baguettes are perfect to dunk into soup. They're also one of my daughter Ella's favorite after-school snacks.

- 1 French baguette (regular or whole wheat), cut crosswise into 4 pieces
- Extra-virgin olive oil, for brushing
- Salt and freshly ground black pepper
- 1 large garlic clove, halved
- 1 cup shredded Comté or Gruyère cheese

1 Preheat the oven to 400°F (200°C). Line a large baking sheet with parchment paper.

2 Slice each piece of baguette in half lengthwise, and arrange the halves on the baking sheet, cut sides up. Brush each piece with oil, and sprinkle with salt and pepper to taste.

3 Bake for 4 to 6 minutes, until the bread is lightly toasted and slightly golden around the edges. Rub each piece of warm bread with garlic. Mound the cheese evenly over the bread. Slide the pan back into the oven, and bake for 2 to 3 minutes, until the cheese is melted. Serve warm.

Garden Ratatouille

PREP TIME: 30 MINUTES
SLOW COOKER TIME: 4–6 HOURS ON LOW *or* 3–4 HOURS ON HIGH

This veggie-packed ratatouille is one of my favorite ways to use up a bounty of summer produce. Fresh tomatoes, eggplant, zucchini, peppers, garlic, and herbs slowly simmer until silky and tender while you play/swim/garden/hike (isn't summer the best?). It's a luscious but light stew that you can serve in a million different ways. Spoon it over creamy cooked polenta or grits (see pages 105 and 177), toss it with cooked pasta, or serve it over chicken or fish. One of my favorite summertime meals is to grill thick slices of rustic bread until lightly charred, top them with the ratatouille, and crumble goat cheese over top. Pour yourself a chilled glass of wine, and *ahhhh*, summer has arrived.

STOVETOP PREP

- 2 tablespoons extra-virgin olive oil
- 1 medium onion, diced
  Salt and freshly ground black pepper
- 3 tablespoons tomato paste

SLOW COOKER

- 3 medium plum tomatoes (about ¾ pound), cored, seeded, and diced
- 1 small eggplant (about ¾ pound), cut into 1-inch dice
- 1 medium zucchini (about ½ pound), cut into 1-inch dice
- 1 medium red bell pepper, cut into 1-inch dice
- 1 medium yellow bell pepper, cut into 1-inch dice
- 6 garlic cloves, lightly smashed
- 3 large thyme sprigs
- 1 rosemary sprig
- 1 tablespoon balsamic vinegar
- 1 teaspoon sugar
  Salt and freshly ground black pepper

- 3 tablespoons chopped basil
- 2 teaspoons lemon juice
- 1 tablespoon extra-virgin olive oil

FOR SERVING

- Cooked polenta, cooked pasta, or toasted thick-sliced bread
- Crumbled goat cheese (optional)

SLOW COOKER JUMP STARTS

Up to 1 day ahead:
Cook the stovetop ingredients and refrigerate.
Chop and refrigerate the tomatoes, zucchini, bell peppers, and garlic (chop the eggplant right before cooking to prevent browning).

RECIPE CONTINUES →

PREPARE THE STOVETOP INGREDIENTS

1 Heat the oil in a medium skillet over medium-high heat. Add the onion and season with salt and pepper to taste. Cook, stirring occasionally, until slightly softened, about 3 minutes. Add the tomato paste and cook, stirring, for 1 minute. (Alternatively, toss everything together in a heatproof bowl, and microwave on high, stirring occasionally, until softened, 4 to 5 minutes). Scrape the mixture into a 4- to 7-quart slow cooker.

ASSEMBLE THE SLOW COOKER

2 Add the tomatoes, eggplant, zucchini, bell peppers, garlic, thyme, rosemary, vinegar, and sugar to the slow cooker. Season with salt and pepper and toss to combine. Cover and cook until the vegetables are tender and silky, stirring once or twice during cooking, 4 to 6 hours on low or 3 to 4 hours on high.

3 Turn off the slow cooker, and pull out the insert (if it is removable). Season the ratatouille to taste with salt and pepper, then stir in the basil, lemon juice, and oil. Let sit for 10 to 20 minutes to allow the flavors to meld (it will also thicken slightly as it cools).

SERVE

4 Serve the ratatouille over polenta, pasta, or toasted bread, and garnish with crumbled goat cheese, if you'd like.

STORAGE
The ratatouille can be refrigerated for up to 5 days or frozen for up to 3 months.

Black Bean Soup + Chipotle Crema

PREP TIME: 30 MINUTES
SLOW COOKER TIME: 7–10 HOURS ON LOW

SERVES
6

I have to admit that until I wrote this book, I was totally indifferent to black bean soup. But when I discovered a bag of black beans in my pantry while I was developing these recipes, I decided to give the soup a try in my slow cooker. Thank goodness I did, as it is now one of my favorites! Dried black beans cook in the slow cooker until perfectly rich and creamy — no soaking required (just be sure to taste for doneness near the end, as the cooking time will depend on the freshness of the beans and the slow cooker you're using). I boost the soup's flavor by incorporating spices, garlic, and jarred salsa. A swirl of smoky and sweet Chipotle Crema takes things over the top. If you have the wherewithal, the soup is especially delicious with the cornbread on page 45.

STOVETOP PREP

- 2 tablespoons extra-virgin olive oil
- 1 large sweet onion, finely diced

SLOW COOKER

- 1 pound dried black beans, picked over and rinsed
- 2 medium carrots, finely diced
- 2 medium celery stalks, finely diced
- 4 garlic cloves, minced
- 1 tablespoon chili powder
- 1 tablespoon ground cumin
- 1 teaspoon dried oregano
- 1 bay leaf
- 3 cups vegetable broth
- 3 cups water
- 1 cup jarred salsa
  Salt and freshly ground black pepper
- 1 teaspoon sherry vinegar

FOR SERVING

- Chipotle Crema (page 56)
- Diced avocado
- Chopped cilantro

SLOW COOKER JUMP STARTS
Up to 2 days ahead:
Cook the onion and refrigerate.
Chop and refrigerate the carrots, celery, and garlic.

RECIPE CONTINUES →

PREPARE THE STOVETOP INGREDIENTS

1 Heat the oil in a large skillet over medium-high heat. Add the onion and cook, stirring occasionally, until slightly softened, about 3 minutes. (Alternatively, toss the onion with the oil in a heatproof bowl, and microwave on high, stirring occasionally, until softened, 4 to 5 minutes.) Scrape the onion into a 4- to 7-quart slow cooker.

ASSEMBLE THE SLOW COOKER

2 Add the black beans, carrots, celery, garlic, chili powder, cumin, oregano, bay leaf, broth, water, and salsa. Cover and cook until the beans are tender, 7 to 10 hours on low (high heat is not recommended).

3 Season the soup generously with salt and pepper to taste (since you haven't added any salt yet, you'll need quite a bit) and stir in the vinegar. If the soup is too thick for your liking, thin it with water as desired.

SERVE

4 Ladle the soup into bowls and swirl in the crema. Garnish with diced avocado and chopped cilantro.

STORAGE
The soup can be refrigerated for up to 5 days or frozen for up to 3 months.

Chipotle Crema

PREP TIME: 5 MINUTES   **SERVES:** 8

This slightly smoky and sweet crema is also amazing on tacos, nachos, or burgers. Freeze the leftover chipotle peppers in their sauce, or use them to make a quick and easy marinade for chicken or steak by puréeing the rest of the can with six garlic cloves.

1 tablespoon fresh lime juice	¼ cup Greek yogurt	1–2 teaspoons adobo sauce (from a can of chipotle peppers)
1 garlic clove, finely grated	1 teaspoon honey	Salt and freshly ground black pepper
½ cup sour cream		

Combine the lime juice and garlic in a small bowl. Let sit for 5 minutes to allow the garlic to mellow. Stir in the sour cream, yogurt, honey, and 1 teaspoon of the adobo sauce. Season with salt and pepper to taste. Taste and add another teaspoon of the adobo if you want more heat.

CHICKEN, TURKEY & PORK

When it comes to dishes my family *craves*, these recipes hit the jackpot. From Thai Curried Chicken and Rice Noodles to Asian Pork Lettuce Wraps to Sticky Ginger Spareribs, these recipes incorporate flavors from around the world into mouthwatering meals that anyone can master. Whether you're snuggling in at home with a rich bowl of soup or entertaining friends with a whole cooked chicken that's way better than rotisserie, the dinners on the following pages are sure to win big.

Chicken Noodle Soup

PREP TIME: 25 MINUTES
SLOW COOKER TIME: 6–8 HOURS ON LOW *or* 4–5 HOURS ON HIGH

What do I make the instant somebody in my family starts sniffling? This soup. Bone-in chicken thighs provide a rich flavor with minimal work (just remove the skin first to prevent the soup from turning too greasy). A Parmigiano-Reggiano rind and onion wedge give the broth an umami complexity. I prefer to cook the noodles separately on the stove when the soup is nearly done, then add them at the end, ensuring that they don't overcook or cloud the broth. On that note, it's best to use a substantial noodle (such as penne or rotini) that can hold up after a few days in the fridge. Serve the soup with a crusty baguette and plenty of softened butter (or with the Skillet Cornbread on page 45), then watch those sniffles disappear.

SLOW COOKER

- 5 medium carrots, sliced ¼ inch thick
- 4 medium celery stalks, sliced ¼ inch thick
- ¼ medium onion, cut into a wedge with the root end intact
- 3 large garlic cloves, lightly smashed
- 2 large thyme sprigs
- 1 bay leaf
- Pinch of red pepper flakes
- 1 (2- to 3-inch) Parmigiano-Reggiano rind
- Salt and freshly ground black pepper
- 3 pounds bone-in chicken thighs, skin removed and discarded, excess fat trimmed
- 6 cups low-sodium chicken or bone broth
- 6 ounces rotini or penne pasta
- 2 tablespoons finely chopped parsley
- 1 tablespoon lemon juice

FOR SERVING

- Freshly grated Parmigiano-Reggiano cheese
- Crusty baguette and softened butter (optional)

SLOW COOKER JUMP STARTS
Up to 1 day ahead:
Chop and refrigerate the carrots, celery, onion, and garlic.
Combine all of the ingredients excluding the pasta, parsley, and lemon juice, and refrigerate.

RECIPE CONTINUES →

ASSEMBLE THE SLOW COOKER

1 Scatter the carrots and celery across the bottom of a 5- to 7-quart slow cooker. Add the onion wedge, garlic, thyme, bay leaf, pepper flakes, and Parmigiano-Reggiano rind. Season with salt and pepper. Arrange the chicken thighs on top, and season with more salt and pepper. Pour in the broth. Cover and cook until the chicken is fork-tender and pulls easily off the bone, 6 to 8 hours on low or 4 to 5 hours on high.

2 In the meantime, cook the pasta according to the package directions until al dente. Drain.

3 Transfer the chicken thighs to a cutting board and let cool slightly. Remove and discard the onion wedge, thyme sprigs, and Parmigiano-Reggiano rind (you can also remove the bay leaf and garlic, if you can find them, although I usually don't worry about them). Coarsely shred the chicken, discarding the bones and cartilage. Transfer the shredded meat back to the slow cooker and add the cooked pasta, parsley, and lemon juice. Season with plenty of salt and pepper.

SERVE

4 To serve, ladle the soup into bowls, and coarsely grate a mound of Parmigiano-Reggiano cheese over the top. I like to serve the soup with big pieces of buttered baguette for dunking (heaven!).

STORAGE

The soup can be refrigerated for up to 5 days or frozen for up to 1 month (I prefer to freeze it without the noodles).

Parmigiano-Reggiano Rinds I always have a chunk of Italian Parmigiano-Reggiano in my fridge, which I freshly grate or shave over pasta, risotto, salads, and pizza. I always keep the rinds — which I store in a bag in the back of my cheese drawer — to throw into soups (including the minestrone on page 21) as well as stews, stocks, and even risotto to impart a nutty flavor.

Thai Curried Chicken & Rice Noodles

PREP TIME: 30–40 MINUTES
SLOW COOKER TIME: 6–8 HOURS ON LOW *or* 4–5 HOURS ON HIGH

This Thai-style chicken soup is cooked in a creamy curry broth for a meal that I *crave*. With garlic, ginger, coconut milk, lemongrass, and curry paste, it's a tad spicy (but mild enough for my kids) and utterly reviving. Turmeric lends a gorgeous yellow color while the bell peppers offer a pop of texture (they're added at the end so that they retain some crunch). The dish is served with loads of fresh herbs, peanuts, and plenty of sriracha, which add essential freshness, texture, and heat. It's a messy, slurpy, soul-satisfying kind of meal. I know it looks like a long list of ingredients, but much of it might already be in your pantry or fridge.

STOVETOP PREP

- 1 tablespoon virgin coconut oil or neutral vegetable oil (such as grapeseed)
- 1 medium onion, finely chopped
  Salt and freshly ground black pepper
- 5 garlic cloves, minced
- 1 tablespoon minced fresh ginger

SLOW COOKER

- 1 quart low-sodium chicken broth
- 1 (13.5-ounce) can coconut milk

- 1 tablespoon plus 2 teaspoons red curry paste
- 2 teaspoons ground turmeric
- 2 tablespoons fish sauce (see the Tip on the next page)
- 1 tablespoon tamari or soy sauce
- 1 teaspoon maple syrup
- 1 lemongrass stalk, trimmed to 6 inches from the bottom (discard the top portion)
- 2½ pounds bone-in chicken thighs, skin removed and discarded, excess fat trimmed
  Salt and freshly ground black pepper

- 2 red bell peppers, finely diced
- 8 ounces ⅛-inch-wide white or brown rice noodles (sometimes called pad Thai rice noodles)
- 1 tablespoon fresh lime juice

FOR SERVING

- Chopped scallions, cilantro, mint, and/or basil
- Chopped roasted peanuts
- Sriracha
- Fish sauce

SLOW COOKER JUMP STARTS
Up to 2 days ahead: **Cook the stovetop ingredients and refrigerate.**
Up to 1 day ahead: **Prep the chicken.**

RECIPE CONTINUES →

PREPARE THE STOVETOP INGREDIENTS

1 Heat the oil in a medium skillet over medium-high heat. Add the onion and season with salt and pepper to taste. Cook, stirring occasionally, until tender, about 3 minutes. Add the garlic and ginger, and cook, stirring, until fragrant, 30 to 60 seconds. (Alternatively, combine everything in a heatproof bowl, and microwave on high, stirring occasionally, until softened, 4 to 5 minutes.) Scrape the mixture into a 5- to 7-quart slow cooker.

ASSEMBLE THE SLOW COOKER

2 Add the broth, coconut milk, curry paste, turmeric, fish sauce, tamari, and maple syrup. Stir to combine. Using the back of a knife, pound the lemongrass all over to bruise it (this will help release its flavors as it cooks). Nestle the lemongrass and chicken thighs into the slow cooker, and season with salt and pepper to taste. Cover and cook until the chicken is fork-tender and pulls easily off the bone, 6 to 8 hours on low or 4 to 5 hours on high.

3 Transfer the chicken thighs to a cutting board. Turn the slow cooker to high (if it's not on high already), and stir in the bell peppers and noodles. Cover and cook until the noodles are tender, 10 to 20 minutes.

4 While the noodles are cooking, coarsely shred the chicken, discarding the bones and cartilage. When the noodles are tender, scrape the shredded chicken back into the slow cooker and cook until heated through. Add the lime juice and season with salt and pepper to taste.

SERVE

5 Divide the curry into bowls and top with a handful of fresh herbs and a sprinkle of peanuts. Serve with sriracha and fish sauce for drizzling.

STORAGE
The curry can be refrigerated for up to 3 days (it will thicken as it chills — thin with water if desired).

Fish Sauce Different brands of fish sauce vary widely in their intensity. I prefer Red Boat brand, which has a clean flavor that's not overpowering. You can find it at specialty grocery stores or online.

Garlic-Lemon Whole Chicken
with Fingerling Potatoes & Fennel + Parsley Pesto

PREP TIME: 30 MINUTES
SLOW COOKER TIME: 4–5 HOURS ON LOW

SERVES
4–6

Slow cooking a whole chicken results in perfectly cooked, juicy meat that's akin to rotisserie chicken. This version is cooked on a bed of fingerling potatoes and fennel for a one-pot meal that's one of our favorite Sunday suppers, especially since the chicken and vegetables cook unattended all afternoon while we play, run errands, or nap (ha, like that ever happens!). The chicken is first rubbed with an herbed butter, then cooked upside down, allowing the breast meat to naturally baste during the cooking process. While the skin helps keep the meat moist during cooking, it's removed at the end, and the meat is served off the bone over the braised vegetables (if you want to serve the chicken with the skin on, transfer it to a baking sheet and broil until browned). A verdant parsley pesto finishes the dish with a splash of freshness (you could also use regular basil pesto). You'll need a 6- to 7-quart oval slow cooker for this recipe.

HERBED BUTTER

- 3 tablespoons butter, softened
- 1 garlic clove, finely grated
- 2 teaspoons lemon zest
- 1 teaspoon finely chopped fresh thyme or ½ teaspoon dried
- ½ teaspoon finely chopped fresh tarragon or ¼ teaspoon dried

  Salt and freshly ground black pepper

SLOW COOKER

- 1 large fennel bulb, halved, cored, and thinly sliced
- 1½ pounds fingerling potatoes, sliced crosswise ½ inch thick
- 3 garlic cloves
- 2 thyme sprigs

  Salt and freshly ground black pepper
- ¼ cup dry white wine
- 1 (4- to 5-pound) chicken, giblets discarded, patted dry

- 1 teaspoon finely chopped fresh tarragon or ½ teaspoon dried

FOR SERVING

- Parsley Pesto (page 69)
- Baguette (optional)

SLOW COOKER JUMP STARTS
Up to 1 week ahead: **Make the herbed butter.**
Up to 1 day ahead: **Rub the herbed butter under the chicken skin and refrigerate.**

MAKE THE HERBED BUTTER

1 Combine the butter, garlic, lemon zest, thyme, and tarragon in a small bowl. Season with salt and pepper to taste. The herbed butter can be refrigerated for up to 1 week or frozen for up to 1 month; bring to room temperature before using.

ASSEMBLE THE SLOW COOKER

2 Place the fennel, potatoes, garlic cloves, and thyme sprigs in a 6- to 7-quart slow cooker. Season with salt and pepper to taste and toss to coat. Pour in the white wine.

3 Using your fingers, gently loosen the skin over the chicken breast and thighs. Rub the herbed butter under the skin, directly onto the chicken meat. Season the chicken all over with salt and pepper to taste. Arrange the chicken, breast side down, on top of the vegetables in the slow cooker (if needed, scoop some of the vegetables from under the chicken to the sides of the slow cooker to help it fit). Cover and cook until the chicken juices run clear and an instant-read thermometer inserted in a breast registers 165°F (74°C), 4 to 5 hours on low (high heat is not recommended).

4 Transfer the chicken to a cutting board, cover lightly with foil, and let rest for 20 to 30 minutes. In the meantime, turn the slow cooker to high and stir the vegetables. Cover and continue cooking the vegetables until the potatoes are tender, 10 to 30 minutes (the time will depend on your slow cooker, so test for doneness occasionally). Stir in the tarragon and season with salt and pepper to taste.

5 Discard the chicken skin, then pull the meat off the bones and shred it into large pieces. Season the chicken with salt and pepper to taste.

SERVE

6 To serve, transfer the vegetables from the slow cooker into shallow bowls using a slotted spoon. Arrange the chicken over the vegetables, and spoon some of the juices from the slow cooker on top. Drizzle with pesto. Serve with chunks of baguette for sopping up all the juices, if you'd like.

 TIP

Chicken Salad For the ultimate chicken salad, chop or tear any leftover meat into bite-sized pieces, then toss it with mayonnaise and a spoonful or two of Parsley Pesto to lightly coat. Spritz the salad with a touch of lemon juice, and season it with salt and pepper to taste. Pile the salad into sandwiches or over salads.

Parsley Pesto

PREP TIME: 5 MINUTES

MAKES: ¾ CUP

Using half water and half oil in this pesto makes for a lighter, less heavy sauce that can be drizzled over the chicken (it's also great over fish or on pasta). This fantastic year-around alternative to basil pesto is also dairy-free. The pesto can sit out at room temperature for up to an hour or can be refrigerated for up to a week (bring it to room temperature and stir before serving).

- 1 garlic clove
- 1½ cups lightly packed parsley leaves
- 3 tablespoons toasted pine nuts (see Tip, page 23)
- 1 tablespoon lemon juice
  Salt and freshly ground black pepper
- ¼ cup water
- ¼ cup extra-virgin olive oil

Drop the garlic into a food processor with the blade running. Add the parsley, pine nuts, and lemon juice, and season with salt and pepper to taste. Process until finely chopped. With the blade running, slowly add the water and oil, and process until incorporated. Season with more salt and pepper if needed. Transfer to a small bowl.

Turkey Meatball Subs +
Spinach, Shaved Fennel & Parmesan Salad

PREP TIME: 20 MINUTES
SLOW COOKER TIME: 2½–3½ HOURS ON LOW *or* 1½–2½ HOURS ON HIGH

The slow cooker is the ideal tool to cook turkey meatballs — it renders them ultratender and juicy even when using lean meat. The meatballs are packed with flavor from garlic, Parmesan cheese, and dried herbs, and I sneak in a bit of added nutrition with finely chopped spinach. They slowly simmer in an easy, homemade tomato sauce (a touch of butter rounds out the flavors and adds body). While you can certainly serve the meatballs over cooked spaghetti, we love to pile them into hoagies with pesto (homemade or store-bought) and mozzarella. It's one of my kids' favorite weeknight meals. The recipe makes four large sandwiches, which you can either serve whole or cut in half to feed eight (it's an awesome game-day appetizer!). The spinach and fennel salad is a crisp and refreshing counterpoint to the hoagies. You'll need a 6- to 7-quart oval slow cooker for this recipe.

MARINARA SAUCE

- 1 (28-ounce) can crushed tomatoes, preferably San Marzano
- 3 garlic cloves, smashed
- ½ teaspoon dried Italian seasoning
- ¼ teaspoon ground fennel seeds (optional)
- ¼ teaspoon sugar
  Kosher salt and freshly ground black pepper
- 1 tablespoon cold unsalted butter, cut into small pieces

MEATBALLS

- 1 pound lean ground turkey
- ¼ cup packed baby spinach, very finely chopped
- 3 tablespoons dried breadcrumbs (regular or gluten-free)
- 3 tablespoons grated Parmesan cheese
- 2 garlic cloves, finely grated
- 1 large egg, beaten
- 1 teaspoon dried Italian seasoning
- ¼ teaspoon ground fennel seeds (optional)
- 1 teaspoon kosher salt
  Freshly ground black pepper

FOR SERVING

- 4 (7- to 8-inch) soft hoagie rolls
- ½ cup Pesto (page 23)
- 4 ounces fresh mozzarella cheese, thinly sliced

SLOW COOKER JUMP STARTS
Up to 1 day ahead:
Assemble the sauce and refrigerate.
Mix together the meatball ingredients and refrigerate in a large bowl.

RECIPE CONTINUES →

ASSEMBLE THE SAUCE

1 Stir together the tomatoes, garlic, Italian seasoning, fennel (if using), and sugar in a 6- to 7-quart oval slow cooker. Season with salt and pepper to taste and scatter the butter over the sauce.

FORM THE MEATBALLS

2 Combine the turkey, spinach, breadcrumbs, Parmesan, garlic, egg, Italian seasoning, and fennel (if using) in a large bowl. Sprinkle with the salt and add pepper to taste. Using a fork, gently stir to incorporate (don't work the mixture too much, otherwise the meatballs could turn tough). Gently form 16 golf ball–sized balls (they'll be sticky), and nestle them in the slow cooker in a single layer. Cover and cook until the meatballs are cooked through and tender, 2½ to 3½ hours on low or 1½ to 2½ hours on high.

MAKE THE SUBS AND SERVE

3 Place an oven rack in the upper third of the oven, and preheat the broiler. Line a baking sheet with foil.

4 Arrange the hoagie rolls on the baking sheet, and spread pesto over one of the cut sides of each roll. Pile the meatballs into the hoagie rolls over the pesto, and top with a couple slices of mozzarella. Broil for 1 to 2 minutes, until the mozzarella is melted. Drizzle a bit more pesto over the top, and serve with tomato sauce from the slow cooker for dunking.

STORAGE
The meatballs can be refrigerated in their sauce for up to 5 days.

Spinach, Shaved Fennel & Parmesan Salad

PREP TIME: 10 MINUTES

SERVES: 4–6

This crunchy and bright salad is the perfect way to round out nearly any meal and is especially scrumptious with the meatball sandwiches (one 5-ounce container of spinach is enough for both the salad and meatballs).

- 1 garlic clove, smashed
- 2 tablespoons lemon juice
  Salt and freshly ground black pepper
- 3 tablespoons extra-virgin olive oil
- 1 medium fennel bulb, shaved or very thinly sliced
- 3 cups baby spinach
- 3 tablespoons grated Parmesan cheese

Rub the garlic around the sides of a large salad bowl. Nudge it to the bottom of the bowl, and pour the lemon juice over it. Let sit for 5 minutes to infuse. Season with salt and pepper to taste and whisk in the oil. Pile in the fennel and spinach, and sprinkle with the Parmesan. Season with salt and pepper to taste, then toss to coat.

Chicken Tikka Masala + Garlic Naan

PREP TIME: 20 MINUTES
SLOW COOKER TIME: 3–4 HOURS ON LOW

SERVES
4–6

What could be better than ultratender chicken pieces enrobed in a creamy tomato tikka masala sauce? Nothing, that's what. This slow cooker tikka masala is comfort food at its best, especially when served with garlicky naan bread for mopping up all the sauce. A quick sauté (or microwave) of the aromatics and spices blooms their flavors, making a big impact in the final dish. Be sure to cook the tikka masala on low heat to allow the flavors to fully meld without overcooking the chicken. For a dairy-free version, use full-fat coconut milk instead of the heavy cream.

SPICE MIX
- 2 teaspoons ground cumin
- 2 teaspoons ground coriander
- 2 teaspoons paprika
- 1 teaspoon garam masala
- 1 teaspoon curry powder
- ¼ teaspoon cayenne pepper
- 3 green cardamom pods, lightly cracked with the back of a knife

STOVETOP PREP
- 1 tablespoon neutral vegetable oil (such as grapeseed)
- 1 medium onion, finely chopped

Salt and freshly ground black pepper
- 2 garlic cloves, minced
- 1 tablespoon minced fresh ginger
- 2 tablespoons tomato paste

SLOW COOKER
- 1 cup canned tomato purée
- 1 teaspoon sugar
- 2 pounds boneless, skinless chicken thighs, cut into 1½-inch pieces

Salt and freshly ground black pepper

- ¼ cup plus 2 tablespoons heavy cream
- 2 tablespoons finely chopped cilantro

FOR SERVING
- Cooked rice or quinoa
- Chopped cilantro
- Garlic Naan (page 77)

SLOW COOKER JUMP STARTS

Up to 2 days ahead:
Mix together the spice mix.
Cook the stovetop ingredients and refrigerate.

RECIPE CONTINUES →

MAKE THE SPICE MIX

1 Combine the cumin, coriander, paprika, garam masala, curry powder, cayenne, and cardamom in a small bowl.

PREPARE THE STOVETOP INGREDIENTS

2 Heat the oil in a medium skillet over medium-high heat. Add the onion and season with salt and pepper to taste. Cook, stirring occasionally, until slightly softened, 2 to 3 minutes. Add the garlic, ginger, tomato paste, and spice mix. Cook, stirring, until fragrant, 30 to 60 seconds. (Alternatively, combine everything, including the spice mix, in a heatproof bowl, season with salt and pepper to taste, and microwave on high, stirring occasionally, until softened, 4 to 5 minutes.) Scrape the mixture into a 4- to 7-quart slow cooker.

ASSEMBLE THE SLOW COOKER

3 Add the tomato purée, sugar, and chicken, and season with salt and pepper to taste. Stir to combine. Cover and cook until the chicken is cooked through and tender, 3 to 4 hours on low (high heat is not recommended). Stir in the heavy cream, and cook until warmed through, about 5 minutes. Add the cilantro and season with salt and pepper to taste.

SERVE

4 Spoon the tikka masala over cooked rice and sprinkle with cilantro. Serve with the naan.

STORAGE
The Chicken Tikka Masala can be refrigerated for up to 5 days.

Garlic Naan

PREP TIME: 5 MINUTES
COOK TIME: 5 MINUTES

SERVES: 4–6

Quickly transform store-bought naan into an irresistible (and addictive!) garlic bread to mop up the tikka sauce. The bread is also delicious with the Squash Curry (page 35).

2–4 naan breads	Salt and freshly ground black pepper
2 tablespoons extra-virgin olive oil	1–2 tablespoons finely chopped cilantro
1 large garlic clove, finely grated	

1 Place an oven rack 4 to 5 inches from the heating element and preheat the broiler. Arrange the naan on a large baking sheet.

2 Heat the oil and garlic in a small saucepan over medium heat until bubbling and fragrant, 1 to 2 minutes. Brush the garlic oil over the naan, and season with salt and pepper to taste (you might not need all the garlic oil).

3 Broil the naan for 1 to 3 minutes, until toasted and browned in spots. Sprinkle the breads with cilantro. Cut into wedges and serve.

Chicken & Black Bean Chilaquiles

PREP TIME: 15 MINUTES
SLOW COOKER TIME: 4–5 HOURS ON LOW *or* 2–3 HOURS ON HIGH

SERVES 4

Chilaquiles is a Mexican dish of fried tortillas that are cooked in salsa or mole sauce until the tortillas are softened. If you haven't tried it, you've got to give this easy slow cooker version a try! Chicken thighs are simmered in store-bought green salsa until fork-tender, then are tossed with black beans, sweet corn, and tortilla chips, which slowly meld into the sauce. It's an incredibly delicious interplay of textures and flavors, especially when topped with avocado, scallions, sour cream, and hot sauce. This is one of my husband's all-time favorite weeknight dinners, and it's also fantastic for brunch, especially after a late night out (if you know what I mean!).

SLOW COOKER

2 pounds boneless, skinless chicken thighs, trimmed of excess fat

Salt and freshly ground black pepper

1 teaspoon chili powder

½ teaspoon ground cumin

½ teaspoon packed brown sugar

2 garlic cloves, minced

2 tablespoons minced shallot (about 1 small shallot)

2 cups jarred salsa verde or tomatillo salsa

½ cup drained and rinsed black beans

½ cup fresh or frozen sweet corn kernels

3 heaping cups corn tortilla chips, preferably low-salt

FOR SERVING

- Shredded cheddar cheese
- Thinly sliced scallions
- Avocado slices
- Sour cream
- Hot sauce

ASSEMBLE THE SLOW COOKER

1 Place the chicken thighs in a 4- to 7-quart slow cooker, and season with salt and pepper to taste. Sprinkle with the chili powder, cumin, sugar, garlic, and shallot. Pour the salsa over the top. Cover and cook until the chicken is very tender and pulls apart easily, 4 to 5 hours on low or 2 to 3 hours on high.

2 Using two forks, coarsely shred the chicken in the slow cooker. Add the black beans and corn; cover and cook until warmed through, about 5 minutes. Pile in the tortilla chips, and toss to coat. Cover and cook, stirring occasionally, until the chips are lightly softened, about 5 minutes.

SERVE

3 Divide the chilaquiles between bowls, and sprinkle with cheese and scallions. Top with avocado slices and sour cream, and serve with hot sauce.

STORAGE
The chilaquiles can be refrigerated for up to 1 day.

SLOW COOKER JUMP STARTS
Up to 1 day ahead:
Chop the garlic and shallot and refrigerate.
Measure out the spices and brown sugar.

Sticky Ginger Spareribs +
Napa Cabbage Slaw

PREP TIME: 15 MINUTES
SLOW COOKER TIME: 7–9 HOURS ON LOW *or* 4–6 HOURS ON HIGH

For years, I made ribs only on weekends since they had to slow roast in the oven for hours, but with the help of the slow cooker, I can now make them any day of the week, any season of the year! Here meaty spareribs get coated with Chinese five-spice powder (which can be found in the supermarket spice aisle), garlic, ginger, and brown sugar before slow cooking until succulent and tender. Best of all, in the summer I'm not left with a steaming hot kitchen! Before

serving, I brush the ribs with a sweet and spicy ginger glaze and pop them under the broiler until they're bubbling, sticky, and irresistible (for a classic barbecue version, check out the Tip on the next page). I like to serve the ribs over rice with a light and crunchy Napa Cabbage Slaw alongside. For the most flavor, rub the ribs with the spice rub the day before. You'll need an oval 6- to 7-quart slow cooker for this recipe.

SPICE RUB

- 1 tablespoon five-spice powder
- 1 tablespoon packed brown sugar
- 1 teaspoon granulated garlic
- 1 teaspoon ground ginger
- 2 (2- to 3-pound) racks St. Louis–style spareribs
  Salt and freshly ground black pepper

STICKY GINGER GLAZE

- ¼ cup honey
- ¼ cup ketchup
- ¼ cup tamari or soy sauce
- 2–3 teaspoons sriracha
- 1 teaspoon toasted sesame oil
- 2 garlic cloves, finely grated
- 2 teaspoons finely grated fresh ginger
  Cooking spray or oil for baking sheet

FOR SERVING

- Cooked rice (optional)
- Napa Cabbage Slaw (page 83)

SLOW COOKER JUMP STARTS
Up to 1 day ahead:
Rub the ribs with the spice rub and refrigerate.
Make the glaze and refrigerate.

RECIPE CONTINUES →

RUB THE RIBS

1 Mix together the five-spice powder, sugar, garlic, and ginger in a small bowl. Season the rib racks generously with salt and pepper to taste on both sides, and rub with the spice mixture. At this point you can cover the ribs with plastic wrap and refrigerate them overnight, or you can cook them right away.

ASSEMBLE THE SLOW COOKER

2 Position the rib racks upright in a 6- to 7-quart slow cooker with thicker ends pointing down and the meaty sides facing outward toward the wall (the racks will wrap around the slow cooker and overlap). Cover and cook until the meat is tender when pierced with a knife, 7 to 9 hours on low or 4 to 6 hours on high. The cooked ribs and juices from the slow cooker can be transferred to a baking pan and cooled, then covered tightly and refrigerated for up to 2 days; bring to room temperature before glazing.

MAKE THE GLAZE

3 In the meantime, whisk together the honey, ketchup, tamari, sriracha to taste, oil, garlic, and ginger in a small bowl. Refrigerate until needed.

BROIL AND SERVE

4 Place an oven rack 4 to 5 inches from the heating element and preheat the broiler. Line a large baking sheet with foil, and spray it with cooking spray or brush it with oil. Arrange the ribs, meaty side up, on the baking sheet; discard the cooking liquid.

5 Brush the ribs with about half of the glaze. Broil for 2 to 3 minutes, until the sauce is bubbling and the ribs are lightly browned. Brush the ribs with the remaining glaze, and broil for about 2 minutes longer, until bubbling and browned.

6 Cut the ribs between the bones, and serve them over rice, if you'd like, with the slaw alongside.

Classic BBQ Ribs For a classic barbecue version of these ribs, replace the spice rub with 1 tablespoon smoked paprika, 1 tablespoon packed brown sugar, 2 teaspoons granulated garlic, and 1 teaspoon dry mustard. Brush the ribs with a store-bought barbecue sauce instead of the glaze before broiling.

STORAGE
The broiled glazed ribs can be refrigerated for up to 5 days or frozen for up to 3 months.

Napa Cabbage Slaw

PREP TIME: 15 MINUTES

SERVES: 4–6

This light and crunchy slaw is the perfect counterpoint to the sticky ribs. The vinaigrette can be refrigerated for up to five days.

SESAME-LIME VINAIGRETTE

- 2 tablespoons lime juice
- 1 tablespoon rice vinegar
- 1 teaspoon honey
- 1 garlic clove, finely grated
- ½ teaspoon finely grated fresh ginger
- ½ teaspoon toasted sesame oil
- ½ teaspoon fish sauce
- Salt and freshly ground black pepper
- 3 tablespoons neutral vegetable oil (such as grapeseed)

SALAD

- ½ small head napa cabbage, very thinly sliced
- 1 small red bell pepper, very thinly sliced
- ⅓ cup coarsely chopped roasted and salted peanuts or cashews
- ⅓ cup coarsely chopped cilantro
- Salt and freshly ground black pepper

1 To make the vinaigrette, combine the lime juice, vinegar, honey, garlic, ginger, sesame oil, and fish sauce in a small bowl. Season with salt and pepper to taste. Whisk in the vegetable oil.

2 To make the salad, combine the cabbage, bell pepper, peanuts, and cilantro in a large bowl. Season with salt and pepper to taste. Toss the salad with enough dressing to coat (you might not need it all).

Asian Pork Lettuce Wraps +
Sesame-Scallion Sauce

PREP TIME: 15 MINUTES (PLUS 1 DAY TO CHILL)
SLOW COOKER TIME: 9–10 HOURS ON LOW *or* 7–8 HOURS ON HIGH

SERVES
6–8

This is one of my very favorite dinners to make when we have friends over. It's an unexpected, hands-on meal, and everybody loves it. Succulent shredded pork — seasoned with ginger, garlic, and Chinese five-spice powder — gets served with lettuce leaves for wrapping, along with peanuts, kimchi, cilantro, and a five-minute scallion sauce. I like to serve everything in bowls in the center of the table so that my guests can build their own wraps. If you want

to round out the meal, serve the wraps with jasmine rice on the side — or ditch the lettuce leaves altogether and make rice bowls instead. The meal is hearty enough to savor in a snowy cabin on New Year's Eve yet light enough to devour on the back deck in the middle of summer (trust me, I've done both!). For the best flavor, refrigerate the pork with the spice paste overnight before cooking.

SPICE PASTE
- 2 large garlic cloves, finely grated
- 1 tablespoon finely grated fresh ginger
- 1 tablespoon packed brown sugar
- 2 teaspoons five-spice powder
- 1 tablespoon extra-virgin olive oil

- 1 (3- to 4-pound) boneless pork shoulder roast (also called pork butt), trimmed of excess fat
  Salt and freshly ground black pepper

SLOW COOKER
- ½ cup low-sodium chicken broth
- ¼ cup tamari or soy sauce
  Salt and freshly ground black pepper

FOR SERVING
- 2–3 heads Bibb or butter lettuce, leaves separated
- Sesame-Scallion Sauce (page 87)
- Cilantro leaves
- Chopped roasted peanuts
- Kimchi

SLOW COOKER JUMP START
Up to 2 days ahead:
Rub the pork with the spice paste.

RECIPE CONTINUES →

RUB THE PORK

1 Combine the garlic, ginger, sugar, five-spice powder, and oil in a small bowl. Generously season the pork shoulder on all sides with salt and pepper, then rub it with the spice paste. Transfer the pork to a large ziplock bag or covered bowl, and refrigerate overnight or for up to 2 days.

ASSEMBLE THE SLOW COOKER

2 Pour the chicken broth and tamari into a 4- to 7-quart slow cooker and add the pork shoulder. Cover and cook until the pork is very tender and pulls apart easily with a fork, 9 to 10 hours on low or 7 to 8 hours on high.

3 Transfer the pork to a cutting board, and let cool for 5 to 10 minutes. Using a fork, coarsely shred the meat, discarding any large chunks of fat. Pile the meat into a serving bowl, and moisten it with about ½ cup of the liquid from the slow cooker. Season with salt and pepper to taste.

SERVE

4 Serve the pork with lettuce leaves for wrapping, along with the sesame-scallion sauce, cilantro, peanuts, and kimchi for topping.

STORAGE
The cooked pork can be refrigerated for up to 5 days or frozen for up to 3 months.

Sesame-Scallion Sauce

PREP TIME: 5 MINUTES

SERVES: 6–8

This scallion sauce instantly perks up the pork lettuce wraps. The scallions will soften as the sauce sits (it won't look like much liquid at first, but the scallions will shrink down). The sauce can sit out at room temperature for up to one hour, or it can be refrigerated for up to one day (bring it to room temperature before serving).

- 2 cups thinly sliced scallions (about 2 bunches)
- 1 tablespoon minced fresh ginger

- 2 tablespoons toasted sesame oil
- 2 tablespoons tamari or soy sauce

- 2 tablespoons sherry vinegar
- Salt and freshly ground black pepper

Combine the scallions, ginger, oil, tamari, and vinegar in a medium bowl. Season with salt and pepper to taste.

Pulled Pork Sandwiches +
Red Cabbage & Sweet Corn Slaw

PREP TIME: 15 MINUTES

SLOW COOKER TIME: 9–10 HOURS ON LOW *or* 7–8 HOURS ON HIGH

SERVES
8–10

My friend Tanya lives in Florida and swears by her slow cooker in the sweltering days of summer. She inspired me to start using my slow cooker in the warm months as well, and now it's my secret weapon for getting dinner on the table without heating up our kitchen (plus, who wants to be tied to the stove when the weather is beautiful?). These pulled pork sandwiches are one of our favorite meals in the height of summer but also in the dark days of winter — they're just as delicious after a day at the pool as they are after a day on the slopes. I like to pile a crunchy cabbage and corn slaw right on top of the sandwiches. For maximum flavor, rub the spice mixture over the pork and refrigerate it overnight before cooking.

SPICE RUB

- 1 tablespoon plus 1 teaspoon smoked paprika
- 1 tablespoon packed brown sugar
- 2 teaspoons granulated garlic
- 1 teaspoon ground mustard
- ⅛ teaspoon cayenne pepper
- 1 (4- to 5-pound) boneless pork shoulder roast (also called pork butt), trimmed of excess fat

  Salt and freshly ground black pepper

SLOW COOKER

- 1 medium sweet onion, thinly sliced
- 4 large garlic cloves, thinly sliced
- ½ cup apple cider vinegar
- ¼ cup honey
- ½–1 cup barbecue sauce

  Salt and freshly ground black pepper

FOR SERVING

- Buns
- Barbecue sauce
- Red Cabbage & Sweet Corn Slaw (page 91)

SLOW COOKER JUMP START

Up to 1 day ahead:
Rub the pork shoulder with the spice rub and refrigerate.

RECIPE CONTINUES →

RUB THE PORK

1 Combine the paprika, sugar, garlic, mustard, and cayenne in a small bowl. Season the pork generously with salt and pepper to taste, and rub it all over with the spice mixture. If you have the time, refrigerate the pork in an airtight container or ziplock bag overnight.

ASSEMBLE THE SLOW COOKER

2 Arrange the onion and garlic in the bottom of a 5- to 7-quart slow cooker, and pour in the vinegar and honey. Place the pork on top. Cover and cook until the pork is tender and pulls apart easily with a fork, 9 to 10 hours on low or 7 to 8 hours on high.

3 Switch the slow cooker off, and transfer the pork to a cutting board. Let cool for 5 to 10 minutes. Using two forks, coarsely shred the pork, discarding any large chunks of fat.

4 Using a ladle, skim off enough fat and liquid in the slow cooker to measure 1 cup, then discard. Transfer the shredded pork back into the slow cooker with the remaining liquid and onions, and add the barbecue sauce to taste. Season with salt and pepper to taste, then toss to combine.

SERVE

5 Pile the pulled pork into buns, and serve with additional barbecue sauce on the side for drizzling. Serve the slaw either in the sandwiches or on the side (or both!).

STORAGE
The pulled pork can be refrigerated for up to 5 days or frozen for up to 3 months.

Red Cabbage & Sweet Corn Slaw

PREP TIME: 15 MINUTES

SERVES: 6–8

This classic slaw gets a pop of color and sweetness from sweet corn. You can use raw kernels off the cob, leftover cooked corn, or even defrosted frozen corn. The slaw holds up well and can be refrigerated for several days.

- ½ cup mayonnaise
- 2 tablespoons apple cider vinegar
- 1 garlic clove, finely grated

- 1 teaspoon honey
  Salt and freshly ground black pepper
- ½ medium red cabbage, cored and very thinly sliced

- 2 cups raw or cooked sweet corn kernels
- 3 scallions, thinly sliced

Whisk together the mayonnaise, vinegar, garlic, and honey in a large bowl. Season with salt and pepper to taste. Fold in the cabbage, corn, and scallions. Season again with salt and pepper to taste.

Carnitas Tacos +
Quick Pickled Red Onions

PREP TIME: 15 MINUTES (PLUS 1 DAY TO CHILL)
SLOW COOKER TIME: 9–10 HOURS ON LOW *or* 7–8 HOURS ON HIGH

SERVES
6–8

With less than 30 minutes of hands-on time, carnitas ("little meats") are slow food at its fastest, and I think you're going to love them in these tacos (in fact, this is one of the most popular recipes on my blog). You'll need to start the meat the day before by rubbing a pork shoulder (also known as pork butt) with a spice paste to let the flavors infuse. The next day, the roast goes into a slow cooker with orange juice, and it gently braises away until the meat is falling apart and tender. Stuff the pork into tortillas with Quick Pickled Red Onions (the Quick Pickled Jalapeños on page 121 are also delicious), buttery avocado slices, salty Cotija or feta cheese, and fresh cilantro. Pass the hot sauce (Cholula, if you've got it), and welcome to heaven.

SPICE PASTE

- 2 tablespoons chili powder
- 1 tablespoon kosher salt
- 2 teaspoons packed brown sugar
- 2 teaspoons ground cumin
- 2 teaspoons ground coriander
- 1 teaspoon dried oregano
- 1 teaspoon ground cinnamon
- 3 garlic cloves, finely grated

- 2 tablespoons olive oil
- 1 (3- to 4-pound) boneless pork shoulder roast (also called pork butt), trimmed of excess fat

SLOW COOKER

- ¾–1 cup fresh orange juice (from 2 large navel oranges)
- Juice from ½ lime (or more to taste)
- Salt and freshly ground black pepper

FOR SERVING

- Warm corn tortillas
- Quick Pickled Red Onions (page 95)
- Cotija or feta cheese
- Avocado slices
- Cilantro sprigs
- Hot sauce

SLOW COOKER JUMP START
Up to 1 day ahead:
Rub the pork shoulder with the spice paste and refrigerate.

RECIPE CONTINUES →

RUB THE PORK

1 Combine the chili powder, salt, sugar, cumin, coriander, oregano, cinnamon, garlic, and oil in a small bowl. Stir to make a paste. Rub the paste all over the pork shoulder. Put the pork in a covered dish or in a large zip-lock bag and refrigerate overnight.

ASSEMBLE THE SLOW COOKER

2 Place the pork in a 4- to 7-quart slow cooker, and pour the orange juice around it (not over the top). Cover and cook until the pork is very tender and pulls apart easily with a fork, 9 to 10 hours on low or 7 to 8 hours on high.

3 Transfer the pork to a cutting board or platter. Pour the liquid from the slow cooker into a medium pot, and allow the fat to settle to the top (alternatively, pour the liquid into a fat separator). Ladle off and discard the fat (there might be quite a lot). Bring the remaining juices to a boil. Cook until slightly syrupy, 10 to 15 minutes — if you run a spatula along the bottom of the pot, you should be able to see a line. Remove the pot from the heat.

4 Using two forks, shred the pork into bite-sized (or slightly larger) pieces. Discard any large chunks of fat. Scrape the shredded meat into the pot with the reduced juices, and toss to coat (you can also scrape everything back into the slow cooker to keep warm). Squeeze in the lime juice, and season well with salt and pepper.

SERVE

5 Serve the carnitas in warm corn tortillas with the pickled onions, crumbled Cotija cheese, avocado slices, cilantro, and a drizzle of hot sauce.

STORAGE
The carnitas can be refrigerated for up to 5 days or frozen for up to 3 months.

Make It Crispy Traditionally, after the pork is shredded, the carnitas are cooked over high heat to crisp up. If you prefer those crispy bits, you can spread the carnitas in a baking pan and broil them until browned.

Quick Pickled Red Onions

PREP TIME: 10 MINUTES, PLUS 30–60 MINUTES TO SIT   **MAKES:** ABOUT 2 CUPS

These zippy onions provide a crunchy and refreshing contrast to the pork carnitas (use leftovers on burgers or sandwiches or in salads). The longer they sit, the more flavorful they become.

1 large red onion, halved and thinly sliced

1 cup apple cider vinegar

1½ tablespoons sugar

1½ teaspoons salt

1 cinnamon stick

½ teaspoon black peppercorns

5 allspice berries

1 Rinse the onion slices well under hot water. Shake dry and put them in a large heat-proof bowl.

2 Bring the vinegar, sugar, salt, cinnamon stick, peppercorns, and allspice berries to a rolling boil over medium heat in a small saucepan, stirring to dissolve the sugar and salt. Pour the hot vinegar mixture over the onion slices, and toss (the liquid won't initially cover the onions, but that's okay: the onions will shrink down). Let sit at room temperature, stirring occasionally, for 30 to 60 minutes, or refrigerate for up to 2 weeks.

3

BEEF & LAMB

When it comes to entertaining, my slow cooker is queen — I can start a meal in the morning, freeing me up to tackle the other items on my list before my guests arrive. Even better, all of these recipes can be completely cooked ahead of time and reheated before serving (in fact, they often get even better with age). It's entertaining at its easiest, but that doesn't mean it's boring. These meals are packed with flavor, from the Sriracha-Braised Brisket to Moroccan Lamb Shanks, Bibimbap Beef Bowls, and my favorite Lamb Ragù. So go ahead and invite the neighbors — dinner is practically done.

Best Beef Chili +
Jalapeño-Cheddar Spoon Bread Muffins

PREP TIME: 20 MINUTES
SLOW COOKER TIME: 6–7 HOURS ON LOW *or* 3–4 HOURS ON HIGH

This is my favorite beef chili. It's reminiscent of the versions I grew up with in the Midwest but with an amplified, richer flavor that I crave every snow day, game day, or plain ol' Sunday. I know it looks like a lot of ingredients, but they're mostly things you'll have in your pantry and spice cabinet. A chipotle chile gives the chili a kick of spice, maple syrup lends sweetness, tamari (or soy sauce) imparts savory "umami-ness," and beer's pleasant bitterness balances everything out. The Jalapeño-Cheddar Spoon Bread Muffins, which are packed with juicy corn kernels and spicy jalapeños, are perfect for dunking (the Skillet Cornbread on page 45 or simple store-bought tortilla chips are also favorite accompaniments). This chili is even better the next day.

STOVETOP PREP

- 2 tablespoons extra-virgin olive oil
- 2 pounds ground beef
  Salt and freshly ground black pepper
- 1 large onion, finely diced
- 2 medium carrots, finely diced
- 4 garlic cloves, minced
- 1 jalapeño, seeded and minced

SLOW COOKER

- 1 (28-ounce) can fire-roasted diced tomatoes
- 1 cup strained tomatoes (such as Pomi brand)
- 1 cup beer (lager or pale ale)
- 1 (15-ounce) can black beans, drained and rinsed
- 1 canned chipotle chile, finely chopped
- 2 tablespoons maple syrup
- 1 tablespoon tamari or soy sauce
- 2 tablespoons chili powder
- 2 teaspoons ground cumin
- 1 teaspoon dried oregano
- 1 teaspoon raw cacao powder or unsweetened cocoa powder
  Salt and freshly ground black pepper

FOR SERVING

- Toppings, such as chopped tomatoes, sliced scallions, shredded cheddar cheese, sour cream, and/or Quick Pickled Jalapeños (page 121)
- Jalapeño-Cheddar Spoon Bread Muffins (page 101)

SLOW COOKER JUMP START
Up to 1 day ahead:
Chop and refrigerate the onion, carrots, garlic, and jalapeño.

RECIPE CONTINUES →

PREPARE THE STOVETOP INGREDIENTS

1 Heat 1 tablespoon of the oil in a large skillet over medium-high heat. Add the beef and season with salt and pepper to taste. Cook, breaking up the meat with a wooden spoon, until browned, 5 to 7 minutes. Drain the meat in a colander or strainer set over a bowl (reserve the skillet).

2 In the same skillet, heat the remaining 1 tablespoon oil over medium heat. Add the onion and carrots, and season with salt and pepper to taste. Cook, stirring occasionally, until the vegetables start to soften, 3 to 5 minutes. Add the garlic and jalapeño, and cook for 1 minute longer.

ASSEMBLE THE SLOW COOKER

3 Scrape the vegetables into a 4- to 7-quart slow cooker, and add the drained beef, diced tomatoes, strained tomatoes, beer, beans, chipotle chile, maple syrup, tamari, chili powder, cumin, oregano, and cacao. Season with salt and pepper to taste and stir to combine. Cover and cook for 6 to 7 hours on low or 3 to 4 hours on high.

SERVE

4 Ladle the chili into bowls, and sprinkle with the toppings of your choice. Serve the muffins alongside.

STORAGE
The chili can be refrigerated for up to 5 days or frozen for up to 3 months.

Jalapeño-Cheddar Spoon Bread Muffins

PREP TIME: 15 MINUTES
COOK TIME: 20–22 MINUTES

MAKES: 12 MUFFINS

These muffins are like the offspring of muffins and spoon bread — they're light and fluffy with a soft texture. You can use raw corn kernels, defrosted frozen corn kernels, or leftover cooked kernels. The muffins can be refrigerated for up to two days or frozen for up to three months.

Cooking spray or oil for muffin pans

1 cup cornmeal

1 cup all-purpose or gluten-free flour

1 teaspoon baking powder

1 teaspoon baking soda

½ teaspoon fine sea salt

1½ cups buttermilk

2 large eggs

¼ cup honey

6 tablespoons unsalted butter, melted and cooled slightly

¾ cup fresh or frozen and defrosted corn kernels

1 large jalapeño, seeded and minced

½ cup shredded cheddar cheese

1 Preheat the oven to 375°F (190°C). Lightly coat a 12-cup muffin pan with cooking spray or oil.

2 Combine the cornmeal, flour, baking powder, baking soda, and salt in a large bowl.

3 Whisk together the buttermilk, eggs, honey, and butter in a separate medium bowl or large measuring cup. Pour the wet ingredients over the dry ingredients, and stir until just incorporated. Fold in the corn, jalapeño, and cheese.

4 Scoop the batter into the prepared muffin cups, and bake for 20 to 22 minutes, until golden on top and a wooden pick inserted in the center comes out clean. Place the pan on a wire rack, and let cool for 5 minutes, then remove the muffins from the pan (if needed, run a small knife around each to release it from the pan). Serve warm or at room temperature.

Braised Short Ribs with Gremolata +
Creamy Parmesan Polenta

PREP TIME: 30 MINUTES
SLOW COOKER TIME: 8–10 HOURS ON LOW *or* 5–6 HOURS ON HIGH

SERVES
4–6

When I entertain, I like to plan menus that can be prepared almost entirely in advance (which is one reason why I love the slow cooker!). This is one of my favorite dinner-party meals since the short ribs can be made ahead — in fact, they taste even better if cooked the day before. The ribs are slowly simmered with tomatoes, wine, and warming spices until succulent and tender,

then they are served over luscious Parmesan polenta. The dish is finished with a sprinkle of parsley gremolata, which wakes everything up. It's an elegant but cozy meal that's always a huge hit. Browning the short ribs first is important for creating a deep flavor, as well as for rendering off some of the fat. You'll need a 6- to 7-quart oval slow cooker for this recipe.

STOVETOP PREP

6–8 meaty English-style bone-in short ribs (4 to 5 pounds), trimmed of fat so that only a very thin layer remains

Salt and freshly ground black pepper

2 tablespoons olive oil

1 medium onion, finely diced

3 large garlic cloves, minced

2 tablespoons tomato paste

1 cup dry red wine

SLOW COOKER

4 medium carrots, cut into 1-inch pieces

1 cinnamon stick

1 bay leaf

2 allspice berries

1 whole clove

1 cup canned or boxed strained tomatoes (such as Pomi brand)

Salt and freshly ground black pepper

GREMOLATA

⅓ cup toasted pine nuts, coarsely chopped (see Tip, page 23)

3 tablespoons finely chopped parsley

1 teaspoon lemon zest

Salt and freshly ground black pepper

FOR SERVING

- Creamy Parmesan Polenta (page 105)

SLOW COOKER JUMP START
Up to 1 day ahead:
Chop the onion, garlic, and carrots, and refrigerate separately.

RECIPE CONTINUES →

PREPARE THE STOVETOP INGREDIENTS

1 Season the short ribs generously with salt and pepper to taste on all sides. Heat the oil in a large skillet over medium-high heat. Working in batches if needed, sear the short ribs on all sides until browned, about 10 minutes total. Transfer the short ribs to a 6- to 7-quart slow cooker, bone sides down (reserve the skillet).

2 Pour off all but about 1 tablespoon of oil from the skillet. Add the onion and season with salt and pepper to taste. Cook, stirring occasionally, until softened, about 3 minutes. Add the garlic and tomato paste, and cook, stirring, 1 minute. Pour in the wine and bring to a boil. Cook until the wine is reduced by about half and the mixture is slightly thickened, 1 to 2 minutes. Scrape the mixture over the short ribs in the slow cooker.

ASSEMBLE THE SLOW COOKER

3 Add the carrots, cinnamon stick, bay leaf, allspice berries, and clove. Pour the tomatoes over the top. Nudge the short ribs so that everything is somewhat evenly distributed. Cover and cook until the meat is fork-tender, 8 to 10 hours on low or 5 to 6 hours on high. Turn off the slow cooker, and carefully remove the short ribs from the sauce. Discard the bones and any large chunks of fat. Using a ladle, skim off the fat from the top of the sauce. Season with salt and pepper to taste.

MAKE THE GREMOLATA

4 In the meantime, combine the pine nuts, parsley, and lemon zest. Season with salt and pepper to taste. (The gremolata can sit at room temperature for up to 1 hour.)

SERVE

5 Spoon the polenta into shallow bowls. Top with the short ribs, then spoon some of the sauce from the slow cooker over each. Sprinkle with the gremolata and serve.

STORAGE
The short ribs can be refrigerated in the sauce for up to 5 days or frozen for up to 3 months.

Creamy Parmesan Polenta

PREP TIME: 5 MINUTES
COOK TIME: 40 MINUTES

SERVES: 4–6

This luscious polenta is a spectacular bed for braised, roasted, or grilled meats and vegetables. Be sure to buy whole-grain polenta or grits (such as Bob's Red Mill brand). You can also make the polenta in a slow cooker — follow the recipe on page 177 for the Cheddar Cheese Grits, swapping out the cheddar for one cup of grated Parmigiano-Reggiano. The polenta can sit at room temperature, covered, for up to one hour. Before serving, reheat it over low heat, adding another splash or two of milk if needed.

- 3 cups water
- 3 cups milk
- Salt

- 1 cup coarse-ground cornmeal (also labeled polenta or grits, not instant)
- 2 tablespoons unsalted butter

- ¾ cup freshly grated Parmigiano-Reggiano cheese

1 Combine the water and milk in a medium saucepan, and bring to a boil (keep an eye on it, as the milk can boil over). Season generously with salt to taste, then whisk in the cornmeal. Bring the mixture back to a boil, whisking constantly. Continue whisking until slightly thickened.

2 Reduce the heat to low and cook, partially covered and stirring often with a silicone spatula, until the polenta is tender and thickened, 25 to 30 minutes. Stir in the butter and Parmigiano-Reggiano. Season generously with salt. Remove the pan from the heat and serve immediately, or drizzle the top with a touch of milk and cover until ready to serve, up to 1 hour (the milk will help prevent a skin from forming).

TIP

Speedy Polenta Hack Nothing can compare to the ultracreamy, fresh flavor of from-scratch polenta, but if you're pressed for time, go for instant polenta instead. It isn't quite as luxurious, but it does the trick. You'll need to follow the instructions on the package, but I find that I usually need to add more milk to prevent a gummy texture (an extra pat or two of butter doesn't hurt, either!). For an even speedier version, buy a premade polenta log (usually found in the same aisle as dry polenta grains), chop it up, and throw it in a pot with milk and water. After a bit of mashing over heat, it will smooth out into a creamy polenta.

Bolognese +
Buttermilk Caesar Salad

PREP TIME: 45 MINUTES
SLOW COOKER TIME: 5–7 HOURS ON LOW *or* 3–4 HOURS ON HIGH

I cook dinner for my extended family every year right before Christmas, and while I've made fancy four-course feasts and expensive roasts, this meal is still everybody's favorite. Unlike the tomato-heavy bolognese sauces you might be used to, this traditional Italian version is made with milk and white wine, giving it a lighter, silkier texture. A mix of pancetta, beef, and pork still makes it feel luxurious, while a touch of balsamic vinegar (which isn't traditional) brightens up the finished sauce. A crisp Buttermilk Caesar Salad is all you need to round out the meal. This Bolognese takes a bit of prep to get going, but once it's in the slow cooker your work is practically done (leaving you plenty of time to wrap those last-minute gifts . . . or is that just me?). It's important to chop the vegetables finely so that they incorporate into the sauce. Also, if you buy prediced pancetta, chop it further until it's minced.

STOVETOP PREP

- 4 ounces pancetta, very finely chopped
- 1 pound lean ground beef
- 1 pound ground pork
  Salt and freshly ground black pepper
- ½ cup tomato paste
- 1 large onion, finely chopped
- 3 medium carrots, finely chopped
- 3 medium celery stalks, finely chopped
- 5 garlic cloves, finely chopped
- 1 teaspoon dried oregano
- 1 cup dry white wine

SLOW COOKER

- 1 cup whole milk
- 1 bay leaf
- 1 teaspoon balsamic vinegar
  Salt and freshly ground black pepper

FOR SERVING

- 1 pound tagliatelle or fettuccine (regular or gluten-free)
- Grated Parmigiano-Reggiano cheese
- Thinly sliced basil
- Buttermilk Caesar Salad (page 109)

SLOW COOKER JUMP START
Up to 1 day ahead:
Chop and refrigerate the vegetables.

RECIPE CONTINUES →

PREPARE THE STOVETOP INGREDIENTS

1 Place the pancetta in a large pan over medium-high heat. Cook, stirring occasionally, until the fat begins to render, 4 to 5 minutes. Add the beef and pork, and season with salt and pepper to taste. Cook, breaking up the meat with a wooden spoon, until the meat is mostly cooked through with some pink remaining, 5 to 7 minutes. Add the tomato paste and cook, stirring, 1 minute longer. Transfer the meat to a 4- to 7-quart slow cooker (reserve the skillet).

2 Place the skillet back over medium-high heat, and add the onion, carrots, celery, garlic, and oregano. Season with salt and pepper to taste. Cook, stirring occasionally, until the vegetables are softened, about 5 minutes. Pour in the wine and bring to a rapid boil. Scrape the mixture into the slow cooker with the meat.

ASSEMBLE THE SLOW COOKER

3 Stir the milk into the slow cooker and add the bay leaf. Cover and cook until the sauce is thick and rich, 5 to 7 hours on low or 3 to 4 hours on high.

4 Skim off and discard some of the fat that has pooled on the surface of the sauce (you don't need to get it all — leaving a bit of fat will give the sauce body). Stir in the vinegar and season well with salt and pepper to taste.

COOK THE PASTA AND SERVE

5 Bring a large pot of salted water to a boil, and cook the pasta according to the package directions until al dente. Drain.

6 Swirl the pasta into bowls. Ladle the sauce over the top, and sprinkle with grated Parmigiano-Reggiano and basil. Serve with the salad on the side.

STORAGE
The Bolognese can be refrigerated for up to 5 days or frozen for up to 3 months.

Buttermilk Caesar Salad

PREP TIME: 15 MINUTES

SERVES: 6

Nothing tastes better with the Bolognese than a crunchy, creamy Caesar salad, and this lightened-up version is just as satisfying as the original. The anchovy is key for flavor, but you can use just one fillet if you prefer a milder dressing (I go for two, but it's a personal preference). The dressing can be refrigerated for up to five days.

- 1 tablespoon lemon juice
- 1 garlic clove, finely grated
- 1–2 anchovy fillets, rinsed in cold water and finely chopped
- ¼ cup buttermilk
- ¼ cup mayonnaise
- ½ cup grated Parmesan cheese
- Salt and freshly ground black pepper
- 3 romaine hearts, chopped

1 Combine the lemon juice, garlic, and anchovy fillet(s) to taste in a small bowl. Using a mortar or a fork, mash the anchovy until it starts to dissolve. Let sit for 5 minutes to allow the flavors to mellow. Whisk in the buttermilk, mayonnaise, and ¼ cup of the Parmesan. Season with salt and pepper to taste. Refrigerate until ready to serve.

2 To serve, pile the romaine into a large salad bowl and toss with the dressing to coat. Sprinkle with the remaining Parmesan, and season with salt and pepper to taste. Toss lightly, then serve.

Bibimbap Beef Bowls +
Garlicky Bok Choy & Sesame Carrots

PREP TIME: 20 MINUTES
SLOW COOKER TIME: 8–9 HOURS ON LOW *or* 5–6 HOURS ON HIGH

Bibimbap is a Korean rice bowl often containing vegetables, sliced meat, and an egg, which are traditionally cooked in a hot stone bowl and served with gochujang sauce. It's one of my favorite meals ever. Luckily I can re-create the same flavors in my own home kitchen, and this dish has become one of my most-asked-for recipes by friends. Instead of using thinly sliced steak, I use boneless short ribs, which are braised until succulent in a sauce flavored with gochujang (see the Tip on the next page), tamari or soy sauce, garlic, and ginger. The tender meat is served over rice with garlicky bok choy, sesame carrots, store-bought kimchi, and a fried egg (optional). A drizzle of the spicy braising sauce ties everything together (the sauce has a serious kick on its own, but it mellows when tossed with the other components). You'll need an oval 6- to 7-quart slow cooker for this recipe.

BRAISING LIQUID

- ¼ cup low-sodium beef or chicken broth
- ¼ cup canned tomato purée
- ¼ cup gochujang
- 3 tablespoons tamari or soy sauce
- 2 tablespoons packed brown sugar
- 1 large garlic clove, finely grated
- 1 tablespoon finely grated fresh ginger

STOVETOP PREP

- 3½–4 pounds English-style boneless short ribs, trimmed of fat so that only a very thin layer remains
- Salt and freshly ground black pepper
- 1 tablespoon neutral vegetable oil (such as grapeseed)
- ¼ cup rice vinegar

FOR SERVING

- Cooked rice
- Garlicky Bok Choy & Sesame Carrots (page 113)
- Fried eggs (optional)
- Kimchi
- Thinly sliced scallions

SLOW COOKER JUMP START
Up to 3 days ahead:
Make the braising liquid and refrigerate.

RECIPE CONTINUES →

MAKE THE BRAISING LIQUID

1 Whisk together the broth, tomato purée, gochujang, tamari, sugar, garlic, and ginger in a medium bowl or large measuring cup.

PREPARE THE STOVETOP INGREDIENTS

2 Season the short ribs generously with salt and pepper on all sides. Heat the oil in a large skillet over medium-high heat. Working in batches if needed, sear the short ribs on all sides until browned, 7 to 10 minutes total. Transfer to a 6- to 7-quart slow cooker (reserve the skillet).

3 Pour off and discard any fat in the skillet. Carefully add the vinegar, and bring it to a boil over medium-high heat, using a wooden spoon to scrape up any brown bits on the bottom of the pan. Scrape the vinegar over the meat in the slow cooker.

ASSEMBLE THE SLOW COOKER

4 Pour in the braising liquid. Cover and cook until the short ribs are fork tender, 8 to 9 hours on low or 5 to 6 hours on high.

5 Transfer the short ribs to a cutting board, and turn off the slow cooker. Using a ladle, skim off enough fat and liquid from the slow cooker to measure about ⅔ cup and discard (depending on the fattiness of your short ribs, feel free to skim off more fat if needed). Transfer the short ribs back into the slow cooker and cover to keep warm.

SERVE

6 Spoon rice into serving bowls. Cut the short ribs into large chunks, and arrange a few pieces in each bowl. Drizzle the meat with some sauce from the slow cooker. Pile the bok choy and carrots next to the short ribs, and top each bowl with a fried egg, if you'd like. Garnish with kimchi and scallions. Serve the remaining sauce from the slow cooker alongside for drizzling.

STORAGE
The short ribs can be refrigerated in the sauce for up to 5 days or frozen for up to 3 months.

 TIP

Gochujang This fermented Korean chili paste has a complex spicy and slightly sweet flavor. It adds an umami kick to marinades, sauces, and dressings. You can find it at specialty grocery stores or online (if you can't eat gluten, look for a gluten-free brand such as Chung Jung One).

Garlicky Bok Choy & Sesame Carrots

PREP & COOK TIME: 15 MINUTES   **SERVES:** 6

The vegetables can be served warm or at room temperature (they can sit out for up to one hour).

3 tablespoons neutral vegetable oil (such as grapeseed)

2 garlic cloves, thinly sliced

1 large head bok choy, coarsely chopped

Salt and freshly ground black pepper

1 lime, halved

6 medium carrots, thinly sliced on the diagonal

Pinch gochugaru or red pepper flakes

1 teaspoon honey

1 tablespoon toasted sesame seeds

1 Heat 2 tablespoons of the oil in a large skillet over medium-high heat. Add the garlic and let sizzle for about 10 seconds. Pile in the bok choy. Season with salt and pepper to taste and toss to coat. Cook, stirring often, until bright green and tender crisp, 3 to 5 minutes. Squeeze in the juice from one lime half. Scrape the bok choy into a medium bowl.

2 In the same skillet (there's no need to wash it), heat the remaining 1 tablespoon oil over medium-high heat. Add the carrots and season with salt and pepper to taste. Sprinkle with a pinch of gochugaru. Cook, stirring occasionally, until tender and golden, 4 to 5 minutes. Drizzle in the honey and squeeze in the juice from the remaining lime half. Transfer to a medium bowl, and sprinkle with the sesame seeds.

Asian-Style Pot Roast +
Potato Purée

PREP TIME: 25 MINUTES
SLOW COOKER TIME: 8–10 HOURS ON LOW *or* 7–8 HOURS ON HIGH

When temperatures drop to freezing, I make pot roast. For me, it's the ultimate cold-weather meal, and it's one of the few dishes I reserve for winter only (some people look forward to snow and sledding; I look forward to pot roast!). While I like a classic version, I love this Asian-style one even better. A boneless beef chuck roast gently braises in a sauce of tamari, garlic, ginger, miso, and star anise until fork-tender and deliciously fragrant. The meat is served with braised carrots and shallots, which cook right alongside the beef. A creamy (and dreamy!) potato purée is the perfect bed for the meat and vegetables, but they are also tasty with steamed rice. Throw on some music and light some candles — winter just got a whole lot more delicious.

BRAISING LIQUID

- ¼ cup tamari or soy sauce
- ¼ cup low-sodium beef broth
- 1 tablespoon honey
- 3 garlic cloves, minced
- 1 tablespoon minced fresh ginger
- 1 tablespoon white miso paste
- ¼ teaspoon red pepper flakes

STOVETOP PREP

- 1 (3- to 4-pound) boneless beef chuck roast, trimmed of excess fat
  Salt and freshly ground black pepper
- 1 tablespoon neutral vegetable oil (such as grapeseed)

SLOW COOKER

- 5 medium carrots, cut into 2-inch pieces
- 4 medium shallots, cut length-wise into quarters (leave core intact)
- 3 whole star anise

FOR SERVING

- Potato Purée (page 117)
- Sliced scallions

SLOW COOKER JUMP STARTS
Up to 3 days ahead: Make the braising liquid and refrigerate.
Up to 1 day ahead: Chop and refrigerate the carrots and shallots.

MAKE THE BRAISING LIQUID

1 Whisk together the tamari, broth, honey, garlic, ginger, miso, and pepper flakes in a medium bowl or large measuring cup.

PREPARE THE STOVETOP INGREDIENTS

2 Pat the roast dry and season it all over with salt and pepper to taste. Heat the oil in a large skillet over medium-high heat. Add the roast and cook, turning occasionally, until browned, 7 to 10 minutes total.

ASSEMBLE THE SLOW COOKER

3 Scatter the carrots, shallots, and star anise over the bottom of a 5- to 7-quart slow cooker. Place the seared roast over the vegetables, and pour the braising liquid over the top of the roast (there won't be much sauce at the bottom of the slow cooker, but that's okay). Cover and cook until the meat is very tender (a thin knife inserted in the center should meet little resistance), 8 to 10 hours on low or 7 to 8 hours on high.

FINISH AND SERVE

4 Using tongs, transfer the beef to a cutting board, and turn off the slow cooker. Let rest for 5 to 10 minutes.

5 Using a ladle or spoon, skim off as much fat as possible from the top of the braising liquid in the slow cooker. Season with salt and pepper to taste.

6 Either slice the roast against the grain, or use a fork to pull the meat into large chunks (discard any large pieces of fat). To serve, spoon the Potato Purée into shallow bowls, and place a few pieces of beef on top. Using a slotted spoon, arrange some of the carrots and shallots from the slow cooker around the meat. Ladle the braising liquid over the top, and sprinkle with sliced scallions.

STORAGE
The pot roast can be refrigerated in the braising liquid for up to 5 days or frozen for up to 3 months.

Potato Purée

PREP TIME: 15 MINUTES
COOK TIME: 15 MINUTES

SERVES: 6–8

These mashed potatoes are light and silky yet rich and comforting. I use a potato ricer to achieve a super-creamy texture, but if you don't have one, you can use a potato masher or fork. The purée can be transferred to a large heatproof bowl, covered with plastic wrap, and set over a pot of barely simmering water for up to two hours before serving.

3 pounds Yukon Gold potatoes, peeled and cut into 2-inch pieces

1 large garlic clove

Salt

4–5 tablespoons unsalted butter

1¼–1½ cups whole milk or half-and-half (or a mix of both), warmed slightly

1 Place the potatoes and garlic in a large pot, and cover with 1 or 2 inches of cold water. Season generously with salt. Bring to a boil. Cook at a gentle boil until the potatoes are very tender when poked with a fork, about 15 minutes.

2 Drain the potatoes, shaking out any excess water. Immediately pass the potatoes and garlic through a ricer (in batches) back into the pot. (Alternatively, transfer the drained potatoes back into the pot, and mash with a fork or potato masher.)

3 Add the butter to taste and stir until mostly melted. Stir in 1¼ cups of the milk until incorporated. If desired, add more milk until you reach the desired consistency. Season with salt (be generous — it makes all the difference!). Cook over moderate heat until the potatoes are hot.

Shredded Beef Mole Tacos +
Quick Pickled Jalapeños

PREP TIME: 20 MINUTES
SLOW COOKER TIME: 7–8 HOURS ON LOW *or* 4–5 HOURS ON HIGH

If you've never made mole before, you *have* to try this! It's an irresistibly complex sauce made with chiles, spices, and chocolate. It has a rich, subtly sweet and spicy flavor that I could bathe in (okay, maybe not literally). While traditionally the sauce can incorporate several dozen ingredients, this simplified version is a cinch to make and can be prepared in advance. The mole simmers with boneless beef chuck until the meat is meltingly tender. The shredded beef is then piled into tortillas with crumbled cheese, avocado, and Quick Pickled Jalapeños, which add a punch of sweet-spicy-vinegary heat. You can also use boneless short ribs or swap out the beef for boneless pork shoulder — just ladle off any excess fat from the sauce.

MOLE

- 2 dried ancho chiles
- ¼ cup raisins
- 1 (14.5-ounce) can fire-roasted diced tomatoes
- ½ medium sweet onion, coarsely chopped
- 3 garlic cloves, smashed
- 2 chipotle chiles in adobo sauce plus 1 tablespoon of adobo sauce from the can
- ⅓ cup toasted sliced almonds
- 3 ounces finely chopped semisweet chocolate (about ½ cup)

- 1 teaspoon packed brown sugar
- 1 teaspoon ground cumin
- ½ teaspoon ground cinnamon
- ⅛ teaspoon ground cloves
   Salt and freshly ground black pepper

SLOW COOKER

- 3–4 pounds boneless beef chuck, trimmed of excess fat and cut into 2- to 3-inch pieces

   Salt and freshly ground black pepper
- 1 tablespoon fresh lime juice

FOR SERVING

- Warm corn tortillas
- Crumbled Cotija cheese or queso fresco
- Avocado slices
- Quick Pickled Jalapeños (page 121)

SLOW COOKER JUMP STARTS
Up to 3 days ahead: Make the mole sauce and refrigerate.
Up to 1 day ahead: Combine the beef and mole sauce and refrigerate.

RECIPE CONTINUES →

MAKE THE MOLE

1 Place the ancho chiles and raisins in separate small bowls, and cover each with hot water. Let sit for 10 minutes. Drain both. Remove and discard the chile stems and seeds. Tear up the chiles and put them in a food processor, along with the drained raisins, the tomatoes and their juices, onion, garlic, chipotle chiles and adobo sauce, almonds, chocolate, sugar, cumin, cinnamon, and cloves. Season with salt and pepper to taste. Process until smooth, stopping and scraping the sides occasionally.

ASSEMBLE THE SLOW COOKER

2 Season the beef with salt and pepper to taste, then place it in a 4- to 7-quart slow cooker. Add the mole sauce and stir to coat the meat. Cover and cook until the meat is very tender, 7 to 8 hours on low or 4 to 5 hours on high.

3 Transfer the meat to a cutting board, and shred it using two forks. Scrape the meat into a large bowl, and add the lime juice and 1 to 2 cups of the sauce from the slow cooker (the meat should be very well moistened in the sauce). Season with salt and pepper to taste. You can either serve the mole immediately or scoop out the leftover sauce in the slow cooker (save it for another use or discard it) and transfer the meat back into the slow cooker. Cover and keep warm until ready to serve.

SERVE

4 To serve, pile the mole into warm tortillas, and top with crumbled cheese, avocado slices, and a few pickled jalapeños.

STORAGE
The shredded beef mole can be refrigerated for up to 5 days or frozen for up to 3 months.

Quick Pickled Jalapeños

PREP TIME: 10 MINUTES

MAKES: ABOUT 1 CUP

These pickled jalapeños pack a lot of spice when eaten on their own, but they lend just the right amount of heat when tucked into the tacos. They're also awesome on the Fish Tacos (page 155) and Carnitas Tacos (page 93) as well as on burgers and sandwiches. They can be refrigerated for up to two weeks.

4 jalapeños, thinly sliced	¼ cup water	1 tablespoon sugar
½ cup apple cider vinegar	1 garlic clove, smashed	¼ teaspoon kosher salt

Put the jalapeños in a small heatproof bowl. Combine the vinegar, water, garlic, sugar, and salt in a small saucepan. Bring to a boil, stirring to dissolve the sugar. Pour the brine over the jalapeños. Let sit at room temperature for 30 to 60 minutes, stirring occasionally. Remove and discard the garlic. Refrigerate until ready to serve.

Sriracha Braised Brisket +
Mashed Sweet Potatoes

PREP TIME: 15 MINUTES
SLOW COOKER TIME: 9–10 HOURS ON LOW *or* 7–8 HOURS ON HIGH

SERVES
6

Every year our friends celebrate an Easter dinner with a big potluck, and my friend Jeff's sriracha brisket is always the first dish to disappear. I've incorporated his flavors into this super-simple but stunning main dish. A spice-rubbed brisket slowly cooks over a bed of onions and garlic with a slightly spicy and sweet sauce. Broiling the brisket at the end creates a delicious crust. I love to serve the sliced or shredded meat over creamy mashed sweet potatoes, which balances out the subtle spice. For the best flavor, rub the brisket with the spice mixture a day or two before cooking. If you want to cook the brisket ahead of time, let it cool in the liquid (before broiling) then refrigerate it for up to three days. Bring it to room temperature (remove any hardened pieces of fat), then broil as directed. See my brisket-buying Tip on page 125! You'll need a 6- to 7-quart oval slow cooker for this recipe.

SPICE RUB

1 tablespoon granulated onion

1 tablespoon granulated garlic

1 tablespoon packed brown sugar

1 teaspoon smoked paprika

1 (4-pound) untrimmed (fat cap intact) beef brisket, cut cross-wise into thirds

Salt and freshly ground black pepper

BRAISING LIQUID

½ cup low-sodium beef or chicken broth

½ cup ketchup

¼ cup sriracha

2 tablespoons packed brown sugar

1 tablespoon tomato paste

1 tablespoon tamari or soy sauce

SLOW COOKER

2 medium sweet onions, thinly sliced

3 large garlic cloves, thinly sliced

3 large thyme sprigs

FOR SERVING

• Mashed Sweet Potatoes (page 125)

SLOW COOKER JUMP STARTS
Up to 2 days ahead: Rub the brisket with the spice mix and refrigerate.
Make the braising liquid and refrigerate.
Up to 1 day ahead: Slice and refrigerate the onions and garlic.

RUB THE BRISKET

1 Combine the onion, garlic, sugar, and paprika in a small bowl. Season the brisket pieces on both sides with salt and pepper to taste (be especially generous with the pepper), then rub them all over with the spice mixture. At this point, you can transfer the brisket to a large ziplock bag or an airtight container and refrigerate it for up to 2 days, or you can proceed with the recipe.

MAKE THE BRAISING LIQUID

2 Whisk together the broth, ketchup, sriracha, sugar, tomato paste, and tamari in a small bowl.

ASSEMBLE THE SLOW COOKER

3 Spread the onions and garlic along the bottom of a 6- to 7-quart slow cooker. Arrange the brisket pieces on top, fat sides up (include any juices from the bag if it was refrigerated). Pour the braising liquid over the meat, and scatter the thyme on top. Cover and cook until the meat is very tender, 9 to 10 hours on low or 7 to 8 hours on high.

BROIL

4 Place an oven rack in the upper third of the oven and preheat the broiler.

5 Transfer the brisket pieces to a cutting board and discard the thyme sprigs. Using a ladle, skim off and discard the fat from the top of the braising liquid in the slow cooker.

6 Using a slotted spoon, transfer the onions and garlic from the slow cooker to a large ovenproof pan (reserve the liquid in the slow cooker for serving). Arrange the brisket on top. Broil for 5 to 8 minutes, until the meat is lightly browned.

SERVE

7 Transfer the brisket pieces back to the cutting board. Scrape the onions onto a large rimmed serving platter. Slice the brisket against the grain (or coarsely shred it), then arrange the meat over the onions. Ladle some of the cooking liquid from the slow cooker over the top. Serve with the sweet potatoes.

STORAGE
The brisket can be refrigerated in the sauce for up to 5 days or frozen for up to 3 months.

Mashed Sweet Potatoes

PREP TIME: 15 MINUTES
COOK TIME: 20 MINUTES

SERVES: 6

Ask me about my favorite comfort food, and I will hand you this recipe. These creamy mashed sweet potatoes are utterly seductive, so you'd better keep the serving dish away from me!

The potatoes can be made up to one day in advance and refrigerated. Reheat them gently on the stove or in the microwave until warmed through.

- 3½ pounds sweet potatoes, peeled and cut into 2-inch pieces
- Salt

- 5 tablespoons unsalted butter, cut into ½-inch pieces, plus more for serving
- 1½–2 cups whole milk or half-and-half

- ¼ teaspoon ground cinnamon
- ¼ teaspoon freshly grated nutmeg
- Freshly ground black pepper

1 Place the potatoes in a large pot and cover with cold water. Season generously with salt and bring to a boil. Cook the potatoes at a gentle boil until they are soft, 10 to 20 minutes.

2 Drain the potatoes, then transfer them back to the pot. Add the butter, 1½ cups of the milk, the cinnamon, and the nutmeg. Season well with salt and pepper. Using hand beaters, beat the potatoes until smooth. If needed, add a few more splashes of milk to thin. If you'd like, top the potatoes with a few thin pats of butter before serving.

TIP

Brisket 101 Brisket comes from the breast of the cow, under the ribs. A whole brisket weighs anywhere from 8 to 20 pounds, but it's often sold broken down into smaller pieces (you can always ask your butcher to cut it). The point cut, also called the second cut, is a triangular piece of meat with lots of marbling. It is often used in traditional barbecue, and it shreds easily. The flat cut, also called the first cut, is a leaner piece of meat that's usually rectangular in shape and slices nicely. You can use either cut for this recipe, but if you select the flat cut, buy a piece with the fat cap intact; otherwise it can be rather dry. Conversely, the point cut will release a lot of fat, meaning you will need to skim much more grease from the surface of the cooking liquid after cooking.

Moroccan Lamb Shanks with Pomegranate & Mint + Cauliflower Couscous

SERVES
4–6

PREP TIME: 30 MINUTES
SLOW COOKER TIME: 6–8 HOURS ON LOW *or* 4–5 HOURS ON HIGH

These ultratender lamb shanks are enrobed in a silky sauce that's fragrant with cinnamon, cumin, coriander, ginger, and allspice. Pomegranate molasses provides a sweet-tart complexity, while cayenne pepper lends a hint of spice. The lamb is served with fresh mint, pomegranate seeds, and pine nuts over a bed of cauliflower couscous, and I think you're going to love the interplay of flavors and textures. This is a meal that will transport you to another land, even if just for dinner. You'll need a 6- to 7-quart oval slow cooker for this recipe.

STOVETOP PREP

4–6 lamb shanks (10 to 12 ounces each)

Salt and freshly ground black pepper

1 tablespoon neutral vegetable oil (such as grapeseed)

1 medium onion, finely chopped

2 tablespoons tomato paste

4 large garlic cloves, minced

1 tablespoon minced fresh ginger

½ cup dry red wine

SLOW COOKER

½ cup canned tomato purée

3 tablespoons pomegranate molasses

1 tablespoon packed brown sugar

2 teaspoons ground cumin

2 teaspoons ground coriander

1 teaspoon ground fennel seeds

¼ teaspoon ground allspice

¼ teaspoon cayenne pepper

2 cinnamon sticks

1 bay leaf

Salt and freshly ground black pepper

FOR SERVING

- Cauliflower Couscous (see page 129)
- Toasted pine nuts (see Tip, page 23)
- Chopped fresh mint
- Pomegranate seeds

SLOW COOKER JUMP-START
Up to 1 day ahead:
Chop and refrigerate the onion, garlic, and ginger (store the onion separately).

RECIPE CONTINUES →

PREPARE THE STOVETOP INGREDIENTS

1 Pat the lamb dry with paper towels, and season with salt and pepper to taste. Heat the oil in a large skillet over medium-high heat until shimmering. Working in batches if needed, cook the lamb shanks until browned on all sides, 6 to 8 minutes total. Transfer to a plate and repeat with any remaining shanks (reserve the skillet).

2 Place the skillet back over medium-high heat and add the onion. Season with salt and pepper. Cook, stirring occasionally, until slightly softened, 2 to 3 minutes. Add the tomato paste, garlic, and ginger, and cook, stirring, until fragrant, 30 to 60 seconds. Carefully pour in the wine, and bring it to a rolling boil, scraping up any brown bits on the bottom of the pan. Scrape the mixture into a 6- to 7-quart oval slow cooker.

ASSEMBLE THE SLOW COOKER

3 Stir in the tomato purée, pomegranate molasses, sugar, cumin, coriander, fennel, allspice, cayenne, cinnamon sticks, and bay leaf. Nestle the lamb shanks and any accumulated juices into the slow cooker. Cover and cook until the meat is fork-tender, 6 to 8 hours on low or 4 to 5 hours on high.

4 Transfer the lamb shanks to a cutting board and tent with foil. Turn off the slow cooker, and let sit for 5 minutes. Skim the fat from the surface of the cooking liquid. Remove and discard the cinnamon sticks and bay leaf. Using a hand blender or a regular blender, blend the sauce until smooth (if using a hand blender, you might need to tilt the slow cooker to pool the sauce). Season with salt and pepper to taste. Transfer the lamb shanks back into the sauce, and turn the heat back on; cook until warmed through, 5 to 10 minutes.

SERVE

5 Spoon the Cauliflower Couscous into shallow bowls or onto rimmed plates. Arrange the lamb shanks over the top, and coat with the sauce from the slow cooker. Sprinkle with pine nuts, mint, and pomegranate seeds. Serve the remaining sauce at the table.

STORAGE
The lamb shanks can be refrigerated in their sauce for up to 5 days or frozen for up to 1 month.

Pomegranate Molasses This is made by boiling pomegranate juice into a sweet-tart syrup. You can find it at most specialty grocery stores (such as Whole Foods Market) or online. It's also delicious in marinades, salad dressings, and sauces or drizzled over pancakes or yogurt.

Cauliflower Couscous

PREP TIME: 10 MINUTES
COOK TIME: 5–10 MINUTES

SERVES: 4

This couscous swaps out the traditional pasta for cauliflower crumbles (also called riced cauliflower), which are now available at most supermarkets in the refrigerated section of the produce department. If you can't find premade crumbles, make your own by pulsing a one-pound head of cauliflower (cut into florets) in a food processor until small, rice-sized pieces form. Cumin, cinnamon, and turmeric lend savoriness to the couscous, while dried apricots, currants, and honey provide sweetness. Feel free to double the recipe if you're feeding a crowd.

- 2 tablespoons extra-virgin olive oil
- 1 pound fresh cauliflower crumbles or riced cauliflower (about 4 cups)
- ¾ teaspoon ground cumin
- ½ teaspoon ground turmeric
- ⅛ teaspoon ground cinnamon
  Salt and freshly ground black pepper
- ¼ cup low-sodium chicken broth
- 2 tablespoons dried currants
- 2 tablespoons chopped dried apricots
- 1 tablespoon honey

Heat the oil in a large skillet over medium-high heat. Add the cauliflower, cumin, turmeric, and cinnamon, and season with salt and pepper to taste. Cook, stirring, until the cauliflower is softened, 3 to 5 minutes. Add the broth, currants, apricots, and honey. Cook, stirring often, until the broth is absorbed and the flavors have melded, 1 to 3 minutes.

Lamb Gyros +
Tzatziki Sauce

PREP TIME: 15 MINUTES (PLUS OVERNIGHT CHILL)
SLOW COOKER TIME: 6–8 HOURS ON LOW *or* 4–6 HOURS ON HIGH

When I was a teenager, my brothers and I loved to order take-out gyros from a strip-mall joint, where the cook would shave long pieces of cone-shaped rotisserie mystery meat onto soft flatbread, then douse it with a yogurt sauce. While I still love gyros, I no longer crave that super-salty meat. Instead, I make my own gyros at home using boneless leg of lamb, which I marinate overnight in lemon juice, olive oil, garlic, dried herbs, and chile flakes. The lamb slowly cooks until it's fall-apart tender, then it gets piled onto flatbreads with a cucumber-and-dill tzatziki sauce, tomatoes, red onion, and feta cheese. It's a brighter, lighter version of that childhood favorite, but it still makes me feel 16 again. Take note that the lamb needs to be marinated overnight. For a richer gyro, use boneless lamb shoulder.

MARINADE

- 3 tablespoons lemon juice
- 3 tablespoons extra-virgin olive oil
- 3 large garlic cloves, finely grated
- 2 teaspoons dried mint
- 2 teaspoons dried oregano
- 1 teaspoon red pepper flakes
- 3 pounds boneless leg of lamb, cut into 2 or 3 large pieces
- Salt and freshly ground black pepper

FOR SERVING

- Soft pita or flatbreads
- Tzatziki Sauce (page 133)
- Diced tomatoes
- Thinly sliced red onion
- Crumbled feta cheese

SLOW COOKER JUMP START
Up to 1 day ahead:
Marinate the lamb and refrigerate.

RECIPE CONTINUES →

PREPARE THE MARINADE

1 Whisk together the lemon juice, oil, garlic, mint, oregano, and pepper flakes in a small bowl. Season the lamb with salt and pepper to taste, and place it in a large ziplock bag. Add the marinade and toss to coat. Refrigerate overnight.

ASSEMBLE THE SLOW COOKER

2 Transfer the lamb and marinade to a slow cooker. Cover and cook until the lamb is fork-tender and pulls apart easily, 6 to 8 hours on low or 4 to 6 hours on high.

FINISH AND SERVE

3 Transfer the lamb to a cutting board, and shred it using two forks. Scrape the lamb into a large bowl, and add ¼ cup of the liquid from the slow cooker to moisten (feel free to add more liquid if desired). Season with salt and pepper to taste.

4 Pile the lamb onto pita or flatbreads along with the tzatziki sauce. Sprinkle with diced tomatoes, sliced red onion, and feta cheese.

STORAGE

The lamb can be cooled in its cooking liquid (before shredding) and refrigerated for up to 1 day (reheat gently, then shred before serving). The shredded lamb can be refrigerated for up to 5 days or frozen for up to 3 months.

Tzatziki Sauce

PREP TIME: 20 MINUTES   **SERVES:** 6

This creamy cucumber-and-dill yogurt sauce is also fabulous on lamb burgers or spooned over fish. Feel free to halve the recipe if you're not feeding a crowd.

- 1 (6-inch) piece English cucumber, finely diced
- ¼ teaspoon kosher salt, plus more for seasoning
- 2 tablespoons lemon juice
- 1 large garlic clove, finely grated
- 2 cups Greek yogurt (whole milk or 2% fat)
- 1½ tablespoons chopped dill
- Freshly ground black pepper

1 Place the cucumber in a colander or strainer and sprinkle with the salt. Toss to coat, then let sit for 15 minutes to draw out some of the water. Transfer to paper towels and pat dry.

2 In the meantime, combine the lemon juice and garlic in a medium bowl, and let sit for 5 minutes. Stir in the yogurt, dill, and cucumbers. Season with salt and pepper to taste. Refrigerate until ready to serve, or for up to 2 days.

Lamb Ragù with Ricotta & Mint

PREP TIME: 30–40 MINUTES
SLOW COOKER TIME: 5–7 HOURS ON LOW *or* 4–5 HOURS ON HIGH

Whether you are going from winter to spring or summer to fall, there's no meal that better bridges the seasons than this lamb ragù. Lamb shoulder (which you can order from your butcher if it's not regularly stocked) slowly cooks with garlic, rosemary, tomatoes, and a hint of cinnamon (which adds a subtle, sweet warmth) until meltingly tender. Partially precooked pasta finishes up right in the sauce, soaking up the fragrant flavors. The pasta is served with a shower of fresh mint and a creamy dollop of fresh ricotta for a hearty meal with a light, sunny taste. You'll want to seek out brands of ricotta without gums or fillers (the ingredient list should list only milk and/or whey, salt, and vinegar). Serve the pasta with the Quick Green Salad (page 27) or the Buttermilk Caesar Salad (page 109).

STOVETOP PREP

- 1 tablespoon extra-virgin olive oil
- 2 pounds boneless lamb shoulder, trimmed and cut into 3- to 4-inch pieces
  Salt and freshly ground pepper
- 1 medium onion, finely chopped
- 1 medium carrot, finely chopped
- 1 medium celery stalk, finely chopped
- 3 large garlic cloves, minced

- 2 teaspoons chopped fresh rosemary
- ½ cup dry red wine

SLOW COOKER

- 1 (28-ounce) can diced tomatoes
- ¼ teaspoon ground cinnamon
  Pinch of red pepper flakes
- 1 bay leaf
  Salt and freshly ground pepper

FOR SERVING

- 1 pound penne pasta
- Salt and freshly ground pepper
- Pecorino Romano cheese, for grating
- Fresh ricotta cheese
- Chopped fresh mint

SLOW COOKER JUMP START
Up to 1 day ahead:
Chop and refrigerate the onion, carrot, celery, garlic, and rosemary.

RECIPE CONTINUES →

PREPARE THE STOVETOP INGREDIENTS

1 Heat the oil in a large skillet over medium-high heat. Season the lamb all over with salt and pepper to taste. Working in batches, sear the lamb pieces until browned on both sides, 2 to 4 minutes per side. Transfer the browned lamb to a 4- to 7-quart slow cooker (reserve the skillet).

2 To the same skillet, add the onion, carrot, celery, garlic, and rosemary. Season with salt and pepper to taste. Cook, stirring often, until the vegetables are softened, about 2 minutes. Pour in the wine and bring to a rapid boil, scraping up any brown bits on the bottom of the pan. Scrape the mixture into the slow cooker.

ASSEMBLE THE SLOW COOKER

3 Add the tomatoes, cinnamon, pepper flakes, and bay leaf. Cover and cook until the lamb is very tender and pulls apart easily, 5 to 7 hours on low or 4 to 5 hours on high.

4 Turn the slow cooker off. Using two forks, finely shred the meat (you can do this right in the slow cooker — pull out and discard any large pieces of fat). Season the ragù with salt and pepper to taste, and cover to keep warm (at this point, the ragù can be cooled, then refrigerated or frozen).

COOK THE PASTA AND SERVE

5 Bring a large pot of salted water to a boil. Add the penne and cook according to the package directions until it is just shy of al dente; it should still be a bit too chewy. Drain and transfer the pasta to the slow cooker. Turn the heat to high, cover, and cook, stirring occasionally, until the pasta is cooked to your liking, anywhere from 5 to 20 minutes, depending on the state of your pasta (taste often!). Alternatively, once you drain the pasta, you can transfer it back into the pot and add the sauce from the slow cooker; this is a good alternative if you make the sauce ahead of time. Cook over low heat, stirring often, until al dente. Season the pasta well with salt and pepper to taste.

6 Spoon the pasta into serving bowls, and sprinkle with grated Pecorino Romano. Top with a dollop of ricotta, and garnish with chopped fresh mint.

STORAGE
The ragù without the pasta can be refrigerated for up to 5 days or frozen for up to 3 months.

4

SEAFOOD

If you're looking for a fuss-free way to perfectly cook fish, then stop here! Cooking seafood in the slow cooker is a huge revelation — the gentle heat is ideal for rendering fish fillets flaky and moist. From spice-rubbed halibut tacos to Tamari-Ginger–Glazed Salmon to Slow-Cooked Cod, preparing fish has never been easier. For stews and curries, such as bouillabaisse and shrimp green curry, the fish goes into the slow cooker at the end, allowing the base to develop a rich flavor first. These are sophisticated but easy meals that might just change the way you cook seafood.

Slow-Cooked Salmon + Cucumber-Caper Yogurt Sauce & Quick Pickled Shallots

PREP TIME: 10 MINUTES
SLOW COOKER TIME: 1–1½ HOURS ON LOW

I think you're going to love this technique for perfectly poaching salmon, adapted from America's Test Kitchen. Salmon fillets slowly cook on a bed of herbs, lemon slices, and white wine until tender and flaky. My mother-in-law introduced me to the cucumber-and-caper yogurt sauce, which is cool, creamy, and utterly divine over the rich fish. Quick Pickled Shallots are my addition and add a burst of brightness to the finished dish. Be sure to check the salmon after 1 hour, as the cooking time will depend on the thickness of the fish and your slow cooker model. I like to serve the salmon with whole grains for a simple but elegant meal. You'll need a 5- to 7-quart oval slow cooker for this recipe.

SLOW COOKER

1 large lemon, thinly sliced

¼ cup dry white wine

1 teaspoon finely chopped dill, plus 2–3 large dill fronds

4 (6- to 8-ounce) skin-on or skinless salmon fillets, 1 to 1½ inches thick, preferably center cut

Salt and freshly ground black pepper

FOR SERVING

- Cucumber-Caper Yogurt Sauce (page 142)

- Quick Pickled Shallots (page 142)

ASSEMBLE THE SLOW COOKER

1 Press a large piece of heavy-duty aluminum foil into a 5- to 7-quart oval slow cooker so that the ends extend over the edge (this will help you pull out the salmon after it's cooked). Arrange the lemon slices in a single layer in the bottom of the slow cooker. Pour in the wine, then add enough water to come just to the top of the lemon slices. Arrange 2 to 3 dill fronds over the lemons.

2 Season the salmon fillets with salt and pepper to taste, and sprinkle with the chopped dill. Arrange the fillets over the lemon slices in the slow cooker, skin side down. Cover and cook until the salmon is tender and flakes easily with a fork, 1 to 1½ hours on low (high heat is not recommended).

SERVE

3 Hold on to the foil handles to transfer the salmon to a large baking sheet. Using a spatula, carefully transfer the fillets to plates. Drizzle with the yogurt sauce, and arrange a few of the pickled shallots on top.

STORAGE
The cooked salmon can be refrigerated for up to 1 day (I prefer to serve leftover salmon cold over a salad).

Cucumber-Caper Yogurt Sauce

PREP TIME: 10 MINUTES   MAKES: ABOUT 1¾ CUPS

This creamy cucumber yogurt sauce with dill and capers transforms the salmon into something special, even it it's an ordinary Tuesday night.

You'll need only six inches of an English cucumber; save the rest for salads or snacking.

- 1 (6-inch) piece English cucumber
- 1 cup plain whole milk yogurt
- 1 tablespoon drained capers
- 2 teaspoons chopped fresh dill
- Salt and freshly ground black pepper

Shred the cucumber on the large holes of a box grater. Transfer the cucumber to a strainer, and press with your hands to remove as much liquid as you can. Scrape the cucumber into a large bowl, and add the yogurt, capers, and dill. Season with salt and pepper to taste. Refrigerate until serving (or for up to 1 day).

Quick Pickled Shallots

PREP TIME: 10 MINUTES, PLUS 30 MINUTES TO SIT   MAKES: ABOUT ½ CUP

Make these pickled shallots after you start the salmon, as they need to sit for 30 minutes. They're also delicious on sandwiches, burgers, salads, and tacos.

- 1 medium shallot, very thinly sliced into rounds
- ¼ cup red wine vinegar
- 2 teaspoons sugar
- 1 teaspoon kosher salt

Place the shallot in a small heatproof bowl. Combine the vinegar, sugar, and salt in a small saucepan, and bring to a boil, stirring to dissolve the sugar and salt. Pour the hot mixture over the shallot and stir to combine. Let sit at room temperature for 30 minutes, or refrigerate for up to 5 days.

Slow-Cooked Cod +
Tomato & Sweet Corn Salad

SERVES
4

PREP TIME: 10 MINUTES
SLOW COOKER TIME: 1–1½ HOURS ON LOW

For a light supper or easy weekend lunch, you can't beat this easy slow-cooked cod. It's especially delicious in the summer when the farmers' market is spilling over with ripe tomatoes and corn on the cob. The cod (or use hake or haddock) slowly cooks until tender and flaky, then gets topped with a juicy salad of tomatoes, sweet corn, fresh herbs, and arugula. Feel free to round out the meal with cooked rice or quinoa — or simply let a glass of crisp white wine do the trick! You'll need a 5- to 7-quart oval slow cooker for this recipe.

SLOW COOKER

- 1 teaspoon lime zest plus 1 large lime, thinly sliced
- ¼ cup dry white wine
- 2 teaspoons paprika
  Pinch of cayenne pepper
  Pinch of sugar

- 4 (6- to 8-ounce) skinless cod fillets, 1 to 1½ inches thick, preferably center cut
  Salt and freshly ground black pepper

FOR SERVING

- Tomato & Sweet Corn Salad (page 144)

ASSEMBLE THE SLOW COOKER

1   Press a large piece of heavy-duty aluminum foil into a 5- to 7-quart oval slow cooker so that the ends extend over the edge (this will help you pull out the fish after it's cooked). Arrange the lime slices in a single layer in the bottom of the slow cooker. Pour in the wine, then add enough water to come just to the top of the lime slices.

2   Combine the lime zest, paprika, cayenne, and sugar in a small bowl. Season the cod fillets with salt and pepper to taste, and sprinkle them with the spice rub. Arrange the fillets over the lime slices in the slow cooker. Cover and cook until the fish is tender and flakes easily with a fork, 1 to 1½ hours on low (high heat is not recommended).

SERVE

3   Hold on to the foil handles to transfer the cod to a large baking sheet. Using a spatula, carefully transfer the fillets to serving plates. Spoon the salad over the top. (The fish and salad are best served the day they are made.)

Tomato & Sweet Corn Salad

PREP TIME: 20 MINUTES

This is one of my favorite summertime side dishes. You can use either raw or leftover cooked sweet corn. It's important to remove the seeds from the tomatoes so that they're not too watery. This salad can sit at room temperature for up to an hour if you reserve the arugula, herbs, and seeds. Add the greens and pumpkin seeds right before serving.

- 1 pound ripe tomatoes, cored, seeded, and finely diced
- ¼ teaspoon kosher salt, plus more for seasoning
- ¼ medium sweet onion, finely diced
- 3 tablespoons fresh lime juice
- 2 tablespoons extra-virgin olive oil
- 1 garlic clove, finely grated
- 3 cups raw or cooked sweet corn (from about 4 ears)
- 2 cups baby arugula
- ¼ cup toasted pumpkin seeds
- 2 tablespoons chopped basil
- 2 tablespoons chopped mint
- Freshly ground black pepper

1 Place the tomatoes in a colander, and toss them with the salt. Let sit for 10 to 15 minutes to drain. Meanwhile, rinse the diced onion in cold water (this helps take away the oniony "bite") and drain well.

2 Whisk together the lime juice, oil, and garlic in a medium bowl. Add the drained tomatoes, drained onion, corn, arugula, pumpkin seeds, basil, and mint. Season with salt and pepper to taste and toss to combine.

Tamari-Ginger–Glazed Salmon +
Quinoa, Edamame & Cucumber Salad

PREP TIME: 10 MINUTES
SLOW COOKER TIME: 1–1½ HOURS ON LOW

**SERVES
4**

This is my husband's favorite salmon recipe, and for good reason — the fillets are brushed with a sweet and salty tamari-ginger glaze before slow cooking to perfection. The fish is served over a quinoa and edamame salad that we nicknamed "sushi salad" since it incorporates pickled ginger, cucumber, and avocado, just like some of our favorite rolls. It's a light and nutritious meal that's ultrasatisfying. I prefer to use skinless salmon fillets (you can ask your fishmonger to remove the skin for you) so that I can serve the fish right over the salad. The salmon is delicious either warm or at room temperature. You'll need a 5- to 7-quart oval slow cooker for this recipe.

TAMARI-GINGER GLAZE

- 2 tablespoons tamari or soy sauce
- 1 tablespoon Dijon mustard
- 1 tablespoon honey
- 1 teaspoon finely grated fresh ginger
- 1 small garlic clove, finely grated

SLOW COOKER

- 1 medium orange, thinly sliced
- 4 (6- to 8-ounce) skinless salmon fillets, 1 to 1½ inches thick, preferably center cut
  Salt and freshly ground black pepper

FOR SERVING

- Quinoa, Edamame & Cucumber Salad (page 149)
- Sliced scallions
- ½ sheet nori (optional)

RECIPE CONTINUES →

MAKE THE GLAZE

1. Whisk together the tamari, mustard, honey, ginger, and garlic in a small bowl.

ASSEMBLE THE SLOW COOKER

2. Press a large piece of heavy-duty aluminum foil into a 5- to 7-quart oval slow cooker so that the ends extend over the edge (this will help you pull out the salmon after it's cooked). Arrange the orange slices in a single layer in the bottom of the slow cooker. Pour in enough water to come just to the top of the orange slices.

3. Arrange the salmon fillets over the orange slices. Season lightly with salt and pepper, then brush generously with the glaze (pour any leftover glaze on top). Cover and cook until the salmon is tender and flakes easily with a fork, 1 to 1½ hours on low (high heat is not recommended).

SERVE

4. Hold on to the foil handles to transfer the salmon to a large baking sheet. Divide the salad among shallow bowls or serving plates. Carefully place a salmon fillet over each salad. Sprinkle with sliced scallions. Using kitchen shears, thinly snip a bit of nori over the top, if you'd like.

STORAGE
The cooked salmon can be refrigerated for up to 1 day (I prefer to serve it cold over a salad).

Quinoa, Edamame & Cucumber Salad

PREP TIME: 30 MINUTES

This refreshing salad is also a lovely side dish to grilled or roasted fish or shrimp. You can cook the quinoa in advance and refrigerate it for up to five days or freeze it for up to three months (or you could use 2¼ cups of leftover cooked quinoa). Find pickled ginger at the sushi counter of your supermarket or in the Asian section.

QUINOA

- ¾ cup quinoa, rinsed and drained
- 1 cup water
- Salt

DRESSING

- 2 tablespoons fresh orange juice
- 2 tablespoons rice vinegar
- 1 garlic clove, finely grated
- ⅛ teaspoon gochugaru or red pepper flakes
- 1 tablespoon neutral vegetable oil (such as grapeseed)

SALAD

- ½ cup frozen shelled edamame beans, defrosted
- ½ cup finely diced English cucumber
- 3 tablespoons coarsely chopped pickled ginger
- 2 scallions, thinly sliced
  Salt and freshly ground black pepper
- ½ avocado, diced

1 To make the quinoa, combine the quinoa and water in a small saucepan. Season with salt to taste and bring to a boil. Reduce the heat to a simmer, cover, and cook until the water has absorbed (you should see little divots in the quinoa), 13 to 15 minutes. Remove the pot from the heat, and let sit, covered, for 5 minutes to steam. Take off the lid and fluff the quinoa with a fork. Transfer to a large bowl and let cool.

2 In the meantime, make the dressing. Combine the orange juice, vinegar, garlic, and gochugaru in a small bowl. Let sit for 5 minutes to allow the flavors to meld. Whisk in the oil.

3 To make the salad, add the edamame, cucumber, pickled ginger, and scallions to the bowl with the quinoa, and season with salt and pepper to taste. Add the dressing and toss to coat (at this point, the salad can be refrigerated for up to 2 hours). Right before serving, fold in the avocado, and season with a touch more salt, pepper, or gochugaru, if needed.

Swordfish Spaghetti +
Fresh Puttanesca Sauce

SERVES
4

PREP TIME: 15 MINUTES
SLOW COOKER TIME: 1–1½ HOURS ON LOW

I must admit that I was never much of a fan of swordfish (which I found rather dry) until I tried cooking it in the slow cooker. It's a game changer! When gently steamed over a bed of lemon slices, white wine, and olive oil, the fish becomes ultratender and juicy — a far cry from the chalky fillets I've encountered in the past. It's especially delicious with this no-cook puttanesca sauce, made with tomatoes, herbs, olives, capers, and a touch of anchovy (which adds dimension, but you won't taste it). The fish and sauce get tangled up with spaghetti for an utterly alluring but light meal. You'll want to make the sauce while the swordfish cooks. This recipe also works great with tuna.

SLOW COOKER

- 1 lemon, sliced ¼ inch thick
- ¼ cup white wine
- ¼ cup extra-virgin olive oil, plus more for serving
- 1 pound swordfish fillet(s), 1 to 1½ inches thick

Salt and freshly ground black pepper
- ½ teaspoon dried Italian seasoning

Fresh Puttanesca Sauce (page 153)

FOR SERVING

- 12 ounces spaghetti
- Salt and freshly ground black pepper
- Good quality extra-virgin olive oil
- Chopped parsley

ASSEMBLE THE SLOW COOKER

1 Press a large piece of heavy-duty aluminum foil into a 5- to 7-quart oval slow cooker so that the ends extend over the edge (this will help you pull out the swordfish after it's cooked). Arrange the lemon slices in an even layer on the bottom of the slow cooker. Pour in the wine, oil, and enough water to come just to the top of the lemon slices. Season one side of the swordfish with salt and pepper to taste and ¼ teaspoon of the Italian seasoning, then flip and do the same on the other side. Arrange the swordfish on top of the lemon slices. Cover and cook until the swordfish flakes easily with a fork, 1 to 1½ hours on low (high heat is not recommended).

2 Hold on to the foil handles to transfer the swordfish to a cutting board, and shred it into large flakes. Place the puttanesca sauce in a large bowl and add the swordfish. Add ¼ cup of the liquid from the slow cooker. Gently toss to combine. At this point, the mixture can sit at room temperature for up to 30 minutes.

FINISH AND SERVE

3 Bring a large pot of salted water to a boil. Cook the spaghetti according to the package directions until al dente. Drain and transfer the spaghetti to the bowl with the sauce and fish. Toss gently to combine. Taste and season with salt and pepper, if needed.

4 Swirl the spaghetti mixture into bowls, and drizzle with a touch of oil. Sprinkle with parsley and serve.

STORAGE
The swordfish spaghetti is best the day it is made, but leftovers can be refrigerated overnight (they make for a great lunch!).

Fresh Puttanesca Sauce

PREP TIME: 15 MINUTES   SERVES: 4

Puttanesca sauce has a rather scandalous history, as it was allegedly created by prostitutes to lure in customers with its strong aromas of garlic, olives, capers, and anchovies. While puttanesca is traditionally cooked, this fresh version uses grape tomatoes for a lively (shall we say seductive?) sauce that's delicious over pasta, fish, or chicken.

2 tablespoons lemon juice

1 tablespoon red wine vinegar

2 anchovy fillets, rinsed, patted dry, and minced

2 garlic cloves, finely grated

3 tablespoons good-quality extra-virgin olive oil, plus more for serving

1 pint grape tomatoes, halved (or quartered if large)

¼ cup finely chopped pitted black olives

2 tablespoons drained and rinsed capers

¼ cup finely chopped parsley

2 teaspoons finely chopped fresh oregano or ½ teaspoon dried

Salt and freshly ground black pepper

Combine the lemon juice, vinegar, anchovies, and garlic in a large bowl. Let sit for 5 to 10 minutes to allow the flavors to mellow. Whisk in the oil. Add the tomatoes, olives, capers, parsley, and oregano, and season lightly with salt and pepper to taste; toss to combine (the sauce can sit at room temperature for up to 2 hours).

TIP

Oil-Cured Olives I love oil-cured black olives in this puttanesca sauce, which lend a meaty, salty flavor. They're dry-cured in salt instead of a brine, then macerated in oil for a few months to help plump up and preserve them. Since they're usually sold whole, you'll need to remove the pits by hand (it's easy!). Use the back of your knife to lightly smash the olives until they crack open, then pop out the pits.

Fish Tacos with Sriracha Mayo +
Lime & Cilantro Slaw

PREP TIME: 10 MINUTES
SLOW COOKER TIME: 1–1½ HOURS ON LOW

SERVES 4–6

I absolutely adore fish tacos, and this version hits all the right marks with spice-rubbed fish, a crunchy lime slaw, and a creamy sriracha mayo. It's the perfect blend of textures and flavors, and you'll be hard pressed to eat just one or two (or three!). They're divine, both in the summer when you're craving lighter fare and in the winter when you're dying for some sunshine. The tacos are also delicious with the Quick Pickled Jalapeños on page 121. Slather any leftover sriracha mayo on sandwiches or burgers. You'll need a 5- to 7-quart oval slow cooker for this recipe.

SPICE PASTE

- 1 teaspoon chili powder
- 1 teaspoon ground cumin
- 1 teaspoon ground coriander
- 1 teaspoon lime zest
- ½ teaspoon packed brown sugar
- ⅛ teaspoon cayenne pepper
- 1 tablespoon extra-virgin olive oil

SLOW COOKER

- 1 large lime, thinly sliced
- 4 (6-ounce) skin-on or skinless halibut fillets, 1 to 1½ inches thick, preferably center cut
  Salt and freshly ground black pepper

SRIRACHA MAYO

- 1 cup mayonnaise
- 1 tablespoon fresh lime juice
- 2 teaspoons sriracha
- 1 garlic clove, finely grated
  Salt and freshly ground black pepper

FOR SERVING

- Warm corn tortillas
- Lime & Cilantro Slaw (page 157)

RECIPE CONTINUES →

MAKE THE SPICE PASTE

1 Combine the chili powder, cumin, coriander, lime zest, sugar, cayenne, and olive oil in a small bowl.

ASSEMBLE THE SLOW COOKER

2 Press a large piece of heavy-duty aluminum foil into a 5- to 7-quart oval slow cooker so that the ends extend over the edge (this will help you pull out the fish after it's cooked). Arrange the lime slices in a single layer in the bottom of the slow cooker. Pour in enough water to come just to the top of the lime slices.

3 Season the halibut fillets with salt and pepper to taste, and rub the spice paste evenly over the top of each. Arrange the fillets over the lime slices. Cover and cook until the halibut is tender and flakes easily with a fork, 1 to 1½ hours on low (high heat is not recommended).

MAKE THE SRIRACHA MAYO

4 In the meantime, whisk together the mayonnaise, lime juice, sriracha, and garlic in a small bowl (feel free to add more sriracha if you like it spicy!). Season with salt and pepper to taste. Cover and refrigerate until you're ready to serve (or for up to 3 days).

FINISH AND SERVE

5 Hold on to the foil handles to transfer the halibut to a large baking sheet. Remove the fish skin if needed, then cut the fish into 2-inch chunks and transfer them to a serving dish.

6 To serve, spread the sriracha mayo on warm tortillas, and arrange a couple pieces of halibut on top. Pile the slaw over the fish.

STORAGE
The cooked fish is best the day it is made, but leftovers can be refrigerated overnight.

Toasting Tortillas Toasting corn tortillas gives them a delicious smoky corn flavor and helps make them pliable. Place the tortillas directly over a gas burner (right on the grate) on medium heat. (Alternatively, on an electric stove, use a preheated cast-iron skillet over high heat.) Cook until toasted around the edges, 30 to 60 seconds. Flip the tortilla and repeat on the other side. Wrap the tortilla in a clean kitchen towel (this is key, as it will allow the tortilla to steam and soften). Keep toasting tortillas, stacking them in the towel as you go (you can toast several at one time using different burners).

Lime & Cilantro Slaw

PREP TIME: 15 MINUTES   SERVES: 4–6

This crunchy slaw is also a perfect match for the Pulled Pork Sandwiches (page 89), Carnitas Tacos (page 93), and Sticky Ginger Spareribs (page 80). It holds up well and can be refrigerated for several days.

- 2 tablespoons fresh lime juice
- 1 garlic clove, finely grated
- ¼ cup mayonnaise
- 1 tablespoon extra-virgin olive oil
- 1 teaspoon honey
- Salt and freshly ground black pepper
- ½ small head green cabbage, very finely shredded
- ⅓ cup coarsely chopped cilantro
- 2 scallions, thinly sliced

1 Combine the lime juice and garlic in a small bowl, and let sit for 5 to 10 minutes so that the garlic mellows a bit. Whisk in the mayonnaise, oil, and honey. Season with salt and pepper to taste.

2 Place the shredded cabbage, cilantro, and scallions in a large bowl. Add the dressing and season with salt and pepper to taste. Toss to combine.

Moroccan Braised Halibut +
Mint & Pistachio Pesto

PREP TIME: 15 MINUTES
SLOW COOKER TIME: 7–8 HOURS ON LOW *or* 4–5 HOURS ON HIGH

With light, flaky halibut and a rich braising liquid, this chameleon of a meal is as comforting as my favorite pair of jeans yet as refined as a silk dress — you could curl up with it at home in sweats or serve it at an elegant party for guests. A hearty base of tomatoes, chickpeas, olives, cumin, paprika, and cinnamon provide the backdrop for perfectly cooked halibut (the trick is to add the fish to the slow cooker at the end, so that it stays moist and flaky). I love to serve the fish and chickpea stew over cooked couscous (or you could use rice or quinoa) to soak up the delicious sauce. An irresistible mint and pistachio pesto provides a burst of fresh flavor and color. If you're running short on time, feel free to use chopped fresh mint instead.

STOVETOP PREP

- 1 tablespoon extra-virgin olive oil
- 1 medium onion, finely chopped
- Salt and freshly ground black pepper
- 4 garlic cloves, minced
- 1 tablespoon tomato paste

SLOW COOKER

- 1½ cups chicken broth
- ¼ cup white wine

- 1 (14.5-ounce) can diced tomatoes, drained
- 1 (14.5-ounce) can chickpeas, drained and rinsed
- 1½ teaspoons ground cumin
- 1 teaspoon paprika
- ¼ teaspoon ground cinnamon
- Pinch of cayenne pepper
- Salt and freshly ground black pepper
- 1¼–1½ pounds skinless halibut fillet, cut into 2- to 3-inch pieces

- ½ cup pitted kalamata olives, halved
- 1 tablespoon lemon juice

FOR SERVING

- Cooked couscous, rice, or quinoa
- Mint & Pistachio Pesto (page 161)

SLOW COOKER JUMP START
Up to 1 day ahead:
Make the braising liquid (without the fish and olives) and refrigerate.

RECIPE CONTINUES →

PREPARE THE STOVETOP INGREDIENTS

1 Heat the oil in a medium skillet over medium-high heat. Add the onion and season with salt and pepper. Cook, stirring occasionally, until slightly softened, about 3 minutes. Add the garlic and tomato paste, and cook, stirring, until fragrant, 30 to 60 seconds. (Alternatively, toss everything together in a heatproof bowl, and microwave on high, stirring occasionally, until softened, 3 to 5 minutes.) Transfer the mixture to a 4- to 7-quart slow cooker.

ASSEMBLE THE SLOW COOKER

2 Add the broth, wine, tomatoes, chickpeas, cumin, paprika, cinnamon, and cayenne. Season with salt and pepper to taste. Cover and cook until the flavors have melded, 7 to 8 hours on low or 4 to 5 hours on high.

3 Turn the slow cooker to high (if it's not on high already). Season the halibut pieces with salt and pepper to taste. Stir the olives into the slow cooker, then nestle in the fish. Cover and cook until the fish is cooked through and flakes easily with a fork, 20 to 30 minutes. Stir in the lemon juice, and season with salt and pepper to taste.

SERVE

4 Serve the halibut over cooked couscous, rice, or quinoa, and spoon the sauce from the slow cooker over the top. Dollop with the pesto, passing any remaining pesto at the table.

STORAGE
The fish and stew are best the day they are made, but leftovers can be refrigerated overnight.

Mint & Pistachio Pesto

PREP TIME: 15 MINUTES

MAKES: ABOUT ¾ CUP

This twist on a classic pesto incorporates fresh mint, parsley, pistachios, and a touch of honey. I think you're going to love it with the halibut, and it's also fabulous with pasta or soups or on sandwiches. The pesto can be refrigerated for up to two days — place a piece of plastic wrap directly on the surface to prevent browning.

- 1 large garlic clove
- 1 cup lightly packed mint leaves
- 1 cup lightly packed parsley leaves and tender upper stems
- ⅓ cup shelled unsalted pistachios
- 1 tablespoon lemon juice
- Salt and freshly ground black pepper
- 1 teaspoon honey
- ½ cup extra-virgin olive oil

Drop the garlic into a food processor with the blade running. Add the mint, parsley, pistachios, and lemon juice, and season with salt and pepper to taste. Process, scraping the sides occasionally, until finely chopped. Drizzle the honey over the top. Slowly pour the oil into the food processor with the blade running, and process until just incorporated. Taste and season with more salt and pepper as needed.

Easy Bouillabaisse +
Garlic Aioli Croutons

PREP TIME: 30 MINUTES
SLOW COOKER TIME: 5–6 HOURS ON LOW *or* 4–5 HOURS ON HIGH

The first time I spooned this saffron-scented bouillabaisse into my mouth, I closed my eyes and sighed. I was transported straight back to Marseille, France, where I visited in my early twenties. I have to admit that I was wary of trying to re-create one of my favorite fish stews in the slow cooker, but I am so happy I did, as this version hits all the right notes while being a hundred times easier to make than the original (meaning we enjoy it year-round, no plane tickets required!). Instead of incorporating

a range of different fish and shellfish as is traditional, I stick with flaky cod (or halibut) and shrimp, which hold up beautifully in the slow cooker. They go in at the very end, after the fennel-and-tomato base has developed its rich flavor. The bouillabaisse is served with Garlic Aioli Croutons for dunking, which provide an irresistible garlicky crunch. Be sure to pass any leftover aioli at the table for spooning straight into the stew.

STOVETOP PREP

- 2 tablespoons extra-virgin olive oil
- 1 large fennel bulb, halved, cored, and thinly sliced

  Salt and freshly ground black pepper
- 5 garlic cloves, thinly sliced
- ¼ cup tomato paste
- ½ cup white wine

SLOW COOKER

- 2 medium carrots, finely chopped
- 2 celery stalks, thinly sliced

- 1 large Yukon Gold potato (about 8 ounces), cut into ½-inch dice
- 1 quart vegetable broth
- 1 (14.5-ounce) can diced tomatoes
- 1 (3-inch) strip of orange zest (removed with a vegetable peeler)
- 3 bay leaves

  Pinch of cayenne pepper

  Salt and freshly ground black pepper

- 1 pound skinless cod, halibut, or haddock fillets, cut into 2-inch chunks
- 12 ounces peeled and deveined shrimp
- ¼ teaspoon saffron

FOR SERVING

- Chopped parsley
- Garlic Aioli Croutons (page 165)

RECIPE CONTINUES →

PREPARE THE STOVETOP INGREDIENTS

1 Heat the oil in a large skillet over medium-high heat. Add the fennel and season with salt and pepper to taste. Cook, stirring occasionally, until slightly softened, 2 to 3 minutes. Add the garlic and tomato paste. Cook, stirring, for 1 minute. Pour in the wine and cook, stirring, until the wine is mostly evaporated and the mixture is thickened, 30 to 60 seconds. Scrape the mixture into a 4- to 7-quart slow cooker.

ASSEMBLE THE SLOW COOKER

2 Add the carrots, celery, potato, broth, tomatoes, orange zest, bay leaves, and cayenne. Season with salt and pepper to taste. Cover and cook until the vegetables are tender, 5 to 6 hours on low or 4 to 5 hours on high.

3 Turn the slow cooker to high (if it's not on high already). Season the fish and shrimp with salt and pepper to taste. Add them to the slow cooker, along with the saffron. Cover and cook until the fish and shrimp are cooked through and opaque throughout, 15 to 20 minutes.

SERVE

4 Ladle the stew into bowls and sprinkle with chopped parsley. Top with the croutons, and serve with any leftover aioli for dolloping.

STORAGE
The stew is best the day it is made, but leftovers can be refrigerated for up to 1 day.

Garlic Aioli Croutons

PREP TIME: 5 MINUTES

This garlic aioli, which is brightened with both lemon zest and juice, wakes up and smooths out the bouillabaisse (use leftover aioli on sandwiches and burgers or as a dip for roasted vegetables or fries). The croutons can be made up to 1 day in advance — store them in an airtight container at room temperature. The aioli can be refrigerated for up to three days.

CROUTONS

- 1 baguette, cut into ½-inch-thick slices
- Extra-virgin olive oil, for brushing
- Salt and freshly ground black pepper

GARLIC AIOLI

- 1 tablespoon lemon juice
- ½ teaspoon lemon zest
- 1 garlic clove, finely grated
- 1 cup mayonnaise
- Salt and freshly ground black pepper

1 Preheat the oven to 375°F (190°C). Line a large baking sheet with parchment paper.

2 Arrange the baguette slices on the baking sheet, and brush the tops with oil. Season with salt and pepper to taste. Bake for about 12 minutes, until golden and crisp. Let cool.

3 In the meantime, make the garlic aioli. Combine the lemon juice, lemon zest, and garlic in a small bowl. Let sit for 5 minutes to allow the flavors to meld. Add the mayonnaise and season with salt and pepper to taste. Whisk to combine. Refrigerate until needed.

4 Before serving, spoon the garlic aioli over the croutons.

Green Curry Shrimp Noodle Bowls

PREP TIME: 20 MINUTES
SLOW COOKER TIME: 5–6 HOURS ON LOW *or* 3–4 HOURS ON HIGH

This aromatic green curry shrimp is one of my favorite meals in spring when we start to crave brighter, lighter flavors. The dish is somewhere between a soup and a noodle dish, so be sure to set the table with both spoons and forks (slurping the noodles is half the fun!). A quick curry base, which is enhanced by store-bought green curry paste, gently cooks with broth in the slow cooker until the flavors have deepened and melded. Coconut milk is added at the end along with quick-cooking shrimp, snow peas, and rice noodles. The snow peas retain their crunch while the noodles absorb the fragrant broth. Depending on the brand of fish sauce you use, you might want to add another tablespoon before serving (different brands vary widely in their intensity). Don't forget the toppings, as they make the dish.

CURRY BASE

- 4 garlic cloves
- 1 jalapeño, halved and seeded
- 1 lemongrass stalk, trimmed to 6 inches from the bottom (discard the top portion)
- 1 medium shallot, coarsely chopped
- 1 (1-inch) piece fresh ginger, coarsely chopped
- 2 tablespoons green curry paste
- ½ cup water

SLOW COOKER

- 1 quart low-sodium chicken broth
- 1 tablespoon tamari or soy sauce
- 1 tablespoon packed brown sugar
- 1 (13.5-ounce) can coconut milk
- 1 tablespoon fish sauce, or more if desired
- 1 pound small to medium peeled and deveined shrimp
- 6 ounces snow peas or sugar snap peas (2 cups), strings removed, cut into ½-inch pieces
- 8 ounces ⅛-inch-wide white or brown rice noodles (sometimes called pad Thai rice noodles)
- 1 tablespoon fresh lime juice
  Salt and freshly ground black pepper

FOR SERVING

- Chopped cilantro
- Chopped basil
- Chopped roasted cashews (see Tip, page 37)
- Sliced jalapeños
- Lime wedges
- Sriracha or hot sauce

SLOW COOKER JUMP START
Up to 1 day ahead:
Make the curry base and refrigerate.

RECIPE CONTINUES →

MAKE THE CURRY BASE

1   Drop the garlic and jalapeño into a food processor with the blade running. Scrape the sides. Peel away and discard the tough outer layer of the lemongrass and trim off the bottom. Finely chop the lemongrass and add it to the food processor, along with the shallot, ginger, curry paste, and water. Process to a paste, stopping and scraping the sides occasionally.

ASSEMBLE THE SLOW COOKER

2   Transfer the curry base to a 5- to 7-quart slow cooker, and stir in the broth, tamari, and sugar. Cover and cook until the flavors have melded, 5 to 6 hours on low or 3 to 4 hours on high.

3   Combine the coconut milk and fish sauce in a small heatproof bowl, and microwave until warm, about 1 minute (alternatively, heat them in a small pot on the stove). Pour the coconut milk mixture into the slow cooker, and stir in the shrimp, snow peas, and noodles. Cover and cook until the noodles are tender and the shrimp are opaque throughout and cooked through, 10 to 20 minutes. Stir in the lime juice, and season with salt and pepper to taste. Taste and add additional fish sauce, if desired (I usually add more, as I prefer a punchier flavor).

SERVE

4   Swirl the shrimp and noodle mixture into bowls. Sprinkle with cilantro, basil, chopped cashews, and jalapeño slices. Serve with lime wedges and sriracha.

STORAGE
The curry noodle bowls are best the day they are made, but leftovers can be refrigerated overnight.

Buying Shrimp Shrimp are sold according to their size (small, medium, or large), with a number designation that refers to the amount of shrimp in a pound. Thus, a larger number will refer to smaller shrimp (there will be more shrimp in a pound). For this recipe, I prefer a small- to medium-sized shrimp — any shrimp with a number designation between 30 and 50 will work well.

5

BREAKFAST & BRUNCH

Whether it's Christmas morning or a lazy Sunday in June, these brunch dishes — including a French toast casserole, a cheesy strata, creamy grits, and a shakshuka with roasted red peppers and artichokes — can simmer away in the slow cooker while you do your thing (I'll take a good book on the couch, please!). They're perfect for hosting guests, and they also just happen to be some of our favorite dinners. For more harried weekdays, a creamy pumpkin and brown rice pudding or the congee can simmer overnight while you sleep, while a rich peach butter and homemade slow-cooked applesauce can be made weeks in advance.

Slow Cooker Congee

PREP TIME: 10 MINUTES
SLOW COOKER TIME: 8–9 HOURS ON LOW

Do you want to cook your breakfast while you sleep? Of course you do! Congee is a savory rice porridge that's often served for breakfast in China, and this ultracreamy version comes together in minutes before bed, then simmers overnight. The key to congee is the bold toppings — I love to drizzle the bowls with tamari, sesame oil, and sriracha, then top them with kimchi, hard- or soft-boiled eggs, chopped peanuts, and scallions. It's a comforting yet enlivening breakfast, and it's also a nourishing dinner. Feel free to add leftover shredded chicken, fish, sautéed greens, or other cooked vegetables.

SLOW COOKER

7½ cups chicken broth

1 cup sticky rice (also labeled sushi rice)

1 (1-inch) piece fresh ginger, thinly sliced

2 garlic cloves, lightly smashed
  Salt

FOR SERVING

- Tamari or soy sauce
- Toasted sesame oil
- Sriracha and/or kimchi
- Hard- or soft-boiled eggs, halved
- Chopped roasted peanuts
- Thinly sliced scallions

ASSEMBLE THE SLOW COOKER

1 Place the broth, rice, ginger, and garlic in a 4- to 7-quart slow cooker and season with salt to taste. Cover and cook on low until the rice is completely broken down and creamy, 8 to 9 hours. Stir well, making sure to scrape the sides and bottom of the slow cooker. For a thinner consistency, add more broth or water (the congee will also thicken as it sits and can be thinned as desired). Season with salt to taste.

SERVE

2 Ladle the congee into serving bowls, and drizzle with tamari, sesame oil, and sriracha and/or kimchi (I usually go for both!). Top the bowls with an egg, and sprinkle with chopped peanuts and scallions.

STORAGE
The congee can be refrigerated for up to 5 days.

Overnight Pumpkin–Brown Rice Pudding

PREP TIME: 15 MINUTES
SLOW COOKER TIME: 8–9 HOURS ON LOW

SERVES
4–6

This brown rice pudding is the perfect make-ahead breakfast, and it tastes just like the holidays! Brown basmati rice simmers overnight with milk, pumpkin purée, warming spices, and maple syrup until tender and creamy with the irresistible flavor of pumpkin pie. Cooking the pudding in a hot-water bath in the slow cooker prevents it from scorching. The pudding is especially delicious when drizzled with half-and-half or cream — or, better yet, a dollop of unsweetened whipped cream (swoon!). A scattering of chopped pecans provides crunch.

SLOW COOKER

- Cooking spray or oil for baking dish
- 3 cups whole milk
- ¾ cup canned or fresh pumpkin purée
- ⅔ cup brown basmati rice
- ¼ cup maple syrup
- ¼ cup packed brown sugar
- 1 teaspoon vanilla extract
- ¾ teaspoon ground cinnamon
- ½ teaspoon ground ginger
- ½ teaspoon fine sea salt
- ⅛ teaspoon ground cardamom
  Pinch of ground cloves

FOR SERVING

- Heavy cream, half-and-half, or unsweetened whipped cream
- Chopped pecans (optional)

SLOW COOKER JUMP START
Up to 1 day ahead:
Measure out and combine the cinnamon, ginger, salt, cardamom, and cloves
(store at room temperature).

RECIPE CONTINUES →

ASSEMBLE THE SLOW COOKER

1 Lightly spray a 1½-quart or similar sized baking dish with cooking spray or rub it with oil.

2 Combine the milk, pumpkin, rice, maple syrup, sugar, vanilla, cinnamon, ginger, salt, cardamom, and cloves in the baking dish and whisk to combine. Cover the baking dish tightly with foil, then place it in a 4- to 7-quart slow cooker. Pour in enough water around the sides of the baking dish to come about a quarter of the way up the sides of the dish. Cover and cook on low for 8 to 9 hours or until the rice is tender. Transfer the baking dish to a heatproof surface, and stir well to combine (it will look strange at first, but it will come together!). Let cool for about 30 minutes to thicken.

SERVE

3 Spoon the rice pudding into serving bowls, and drizzle each with heavy cream, half-and-half, or a dollop of unsweetened whipped cream. Sprinkle with chopped pecans, if you'd like.

> **STORAGE**
> The rice pudding can be refrigerated for up to 5 days.

Cheddar Cheese Grits +
Bacony Greens & Fried Eggs

PREP TIME: 5 MINUTES
SLOW COOKER TIME: 3–4 HOURS ON LOW *or* 2–3 HOURS ON HIGH

SERVES
6

Grits are one of my favorite comfort foods, which is why I was ecstatic to discover that I could make them in my slow cooker. They turn creamy and thick without becoming lumpy or dry. Best of all, they require no monitoring or stirring as they would on the stove! These cheddar grits are a delicious side dish, but I also love to serve them under bacony greens and fried eggs as a full meal. Toasted pepitas provide crunch while hot sauce adds a vinegary heat. If tomatoes are in season, I'll often add a few juicy slices as well. This is definitely one of my favorite brunches, and it also makes for a darn fine dinner. You can transform the grits into polenta by omitting the cheddar cheese and adding a handful or two of grated Parmesan cheese instead (try it with the Braised Short Ribs on page 102).

SLOW COOKER

Cooking spray or oil, for slow cooker

3½ cups water

2 cups milk

1¼ cups coarse-ground cornmeal (also labeled grits or polenta, not instant)

Salt and freshly ground black pepper

1 tablespoon unsalted butter

6 ounces shredded sharp white cheddar cheese (2 cups)

FOR SERVING

- Bacony Greens (page 178)
- Fried eggs
- Toasted pepitas
- Hot sauce

RECIPE CONTINUES →

ASSEMBLE THE SLOW COOKER

1 Spray a 4- to 7-quart slow cooker with cooking spray or rub it lightly with oil. Pour in the water and milk, then whisk in the cornmeal. Cover and cook until the grits are creamy and tender, 3 to 4 hours on low or 2 to 3 hours on high. Stir the grits well, then add the butter and cheese. Season generously with salt and pepper. Cover and keep warm (the grits can sit for up to 2 hours; reheat on low if needed).

SERVE

2 Spoon the grits into shallow bowls, and top them with the greens. Slide a fried egg or two over each. Sprinkle with pepitas and serve with hot sauce for drizzling.

STORAGE

The grits are creamiest straight from the slow cooker, but leftovers can be refrigerated for up to 5 days. Reheat them in the microwave or on the stovetop until warmed through, adding more water to thin as needed.

Bacony Greens

PREP TIME: 15 MINUTES
COOK TIME: 15 MINUTES

SERVES: 4–6

Bacon is to kale like jam is to toast — it's a marriage made in heaven. These greens have just enough bacon to provide flavor without weighing them down. Feel free to swap out the kale for collard greens, Swiss chard, or mature spinach.

- 3 slices bacon, finely chopped
- 1 medium shallot, thinly sliced
- 4 garlic cloves, thinly sliced

- 1 large bunch curly kale, stemmed and coarsely chopped (about 8 cups)
- 2 tablespoons water or broth

- Salt and freshly ground black pepper
- 2 teaspoons apple cider vinegar

Scatter the bacon in a large skillet, and turn the heat to medium. Cook, stirring occasionally, until the bacon has started to crisp up and the fat has rendered, about 5 minutes. Add the shallot and garlic, and cook, stirring, until tender, 1 to 2 minutes. Pile in the kale, add the water, and season with salt and pepper to taste. Cover the pan and cook, stirring occasionally, until the kale is bright green and tender, 3 to 5 minutes (if the pan starts to look too dry, add another splash or two of water). Stir in the vinegar. Season with more salt and pepper as needed. Serve immediately or transfer to a large bowl and cover to keep warm.

French Toast Casserole

PREP TIME: 15 MINUTES (PLUS 1 DAY TO DRY OUT BREAD)
SLOW COOKER TIME: 2½–3½ HOURS ON LOW

This casserole is the perfect way to feed a crowd without having to be stuck at the stove. Challah bread is left out overnight to dry (or you can dry it in the oven — see the Tip on the next page), then it goes in the slow cooker with a quick almond- and vanilla-scented French toast batter. A simple brown sugar, butter, and pecan topping provides crunch. The casserole bakes until the eggs are set and the bread is creamy in the center. Serve it with maple syrup and a bowl of fresh fruit, and let your guests help themselves (now go relax with a mimosa!). Note: don't substitute brioche for the challah, as it won't hold up as well. You will need a 4- to 7-quart oval slow cooker for this recipe.

BREAD

- 1 (15-ounce) loaf challah bread, cut into 1½-inch cubes

SLOW COOKER

- Cooking spray or oil, for slow cooker
- 8 large eggs
- 2¼ cups whole milk
- 3 tablespoons packed brown sugar
- 1 teaspoon vanilla extract
- ½ teaspoon almond extract
- ½ teaspoon ground cinnamon
- ⅛ teaspoon freshly grated nutmeg
- ¼ plus ⅛ teaspoon fine sea salt
- 3 tablespoons cold unsalted butter
- ½ cup chopped pecans

FOR SERVING

- Maple syrup
- Berries (optional)

RECIPE CONTINUES →

DRY OUT THE BREAD

1 Spread the bread onto a large baking sheet in a single layer, and let sit, uncovered, overnight (or for up to 2 days).

ASSEMBLE THE SLOW COOKER

2 Coat the inside of a 4- to 7-quart oval slow cooker with cooking spray or brush it lightly with oil. Add the bread cubes. Whisk together the eggs, milk, 1 tablespoon of the sugar, the vanilla, almond extract, cinnamon, nutmeg, and ¼ teaspoon of the salt. Pour the egg custard over the bread in the slow cooker and press gently to submerge.

3 Shred the butter using a cheese grater, and scatter it over the bread in the slow cooker. Sprinkle on the remaining 2 tablespoons sugar, the pecans, and the remaining ⅛ teaspoon salt.

4 Cover and cook on low until the eggs are set and the bread is tender, 2½ to 3½ hours on low. Turn off the slow cooker, and let sit for 5 to 10 minutes (or for up to 1 hour).

SERVE

5 Spoon the French toast onto plates, and serve it with maple syrup and berries, if you'd like.

STORAGE
The French toast can be refrigerated for up to 3 days. Reheat it in the oven (or in a toaster oven) until warmed through.

TIP **Drying Bread in the Oven** To dry the bread in the oven, spread it on a large baking sheet, and bake it at 250°F (120°C) until it's dry to the touch, about 30 minutes.

Spinach, Prosciutto & Gruyère Strata

PREP TIME: 30 MINUTES (PLUS 1 DAY TO DRY OUT BREAD)
SLOW COOKER TIME: 2½–3½ HOURS ON LOW

SERVES
6

My mom used to make a ham-and-cheese strata on special occasions when I was growing up, and this version, which incorporates leeks, prosciutto, and Gruyère, is deliciously nostalgic with a dash more sophistication. Lining the slow cooker with aluminum foil will enable you to transfer the cooked strata to a platter before serving, making for a lovely presentation. It's the perfect centerpiece for leisurely weekend brunches and holidays, and it's also a delicious weeknight dinner when paired with a green salad. Take note that the bread needs to sit out overnight to dry out (or you can dry it out in the oven — see opposite page). You'll also need to defrost frozen spinach before beginning. I usually pop the spinach in the fridge overnight, or you can defrost it in the microwave. You will need a 4- to 7-quart oval slow cooker for this recipe.

BREAD

- 1 (10- to 12-ounce) baguette, cut into ½-inch cubes (about 7–8 cups)

STOVETOP PREP

- 1 tablespoon extra-virgin olive oil
- 2 medium leeks, white and light green parts only, halved and thinly sliced
- 3 garlic cloves, minced

- 1 tablespoon chopped fresh thyme or 1 teaspoon dried thyme
  Salt and freshly ground black pepper
- 10 ounces frozen chopped spinach, defrosted and squeezed dry between paper towels
- 3 ounces thinly sliced prosciutto, finely chopped

SLOW COOKER

- Cooking spray or oil, for slow cooker
- 8 large eggs
- 2¼ cups half-and-half
- 1 teaspoon kosher salt
  Pinch of freshly grated nutmeg
  Pinch of cayenne pepper
- 6 ounces shredded Gruyère or Comté cheese (2 cups)

SLOW COOKER JUMP START
Up to 1 day ahead:
Cook the leeks, garlic, and thyme, and combine them with the spinach and prosciutto, then refrigerate.

RECIPE CONTINUES →

DRY OUT THE BREAD

1 Spread the bread onto a large baking sheet in a single layer, and let sit, uncovered, overnight (or for up to 2 days).

PREPARE THE STOVETOP INGREDIENTS

2 Heat the oil in a medium skillet over medium heat. Add the leeks, garlic, and thyme, and season with salt and pepper to taste. Cook, stirring often, until softened, about 3 minutes. (Alternatively, toss the oil, leeks, garlic, and thyme in a heatproof bowl, season with salt and pepper to taste, and microwave on high, stirring occasionally, until the leeks are softened, 4 to 5 minutes). Remove the pan from the heat, and stir in the spinach and prosciutto. Season with salt and pepper to taste. Set aside.

ASSEMBLE THE SLOW COOKER

3 Line a 4- to 7-quart oval slow cooker with a large piece of heavy-duty aluminum foil so that the ends extend over the edge (this will help you pull out the strata later). Press another piece of foil into the slow cooker going in the opposite direction (the inside of the slow cooker should now be completely covered in foil). Spray the foil with cooking spray or brush it with oil.

4 Whisk together the eggs, half-and-half, salt, nutmeg, and cayenne in a medium bowl.

5 Spread half of the bread into the bottom of the slow cooker, and sprinkle half of the leek mixture over the top. Sprinkle with half of the Gruyère. Arrange the remaining bread on top, followed by the remaining leek mixture and the rest of the Gruyère. Pour the egg mixture over everything and press down gently. Cover and cook until the eggs are set, 2½ to 3½ hours on low. Turn off the slow cooker, and let sit, covered, for 10 to 20 minutes (or for up to 2 hours).

SERVE

6 Using the foil handles, transfer the strata to a serving platter or a cutting board. Cut it into pieces and serve.

STORAGE
The strata can be refrigerated for up to 3 days. Reheat it in the oven (or in a toaster oven) until warmed through.

Roasted Red Pepper & Artichoke Shakshuka with Feta & Herbs

PREP TIME: 20 MINUTES
SLOW COOKER TIME: 4–6 HOURS ON LOW *or* 2–3 HOURS ON HIGH

Shakshuka is a dish of eggs poached in a tomato sauce, and it's one of our favorite weekend brunches *or* easy weeknight dinners. This version incorporates roasted red peppers, artichoke hearts, cumin, and smoked paprika and is finished with fresh herbs and crumbled feta. The creamy cheese, bright herbs, robust sauce, and rich egg yolk create a sigh-worthy bite, especially if mopped up with a crusty baguette or piece of soft pita bread. If I'm making this for brunch, I prep everything the day before right in my slow cooker (without the eggs), refrigerate the insert overnight, then start the slow cooker in the morning when I wake up.

STOVETOP PREP

- 1 tablespoon extra-virgin olive oil
- ½ medium red onion, thinly sliced
- 3 garlic cloves, thinly sliced
  Salt and freshly ground black pepper
- 1 tablespoon tomato paste

SLOW COOKER

- 1 (28-ounce) can diced tomatoes
- 1 cup sliced jarred roasted red peppers
- 1 (8.5-ounce) can whole artichoke hearts in water, drained, patted dry, and halved
- 1 tablespoon extra-virgin olive oil
- 1 teaspoon ground cumin
- ¾ teaspoon sugar
- ½ teaspoon smoked paprika
  Pinch of cayenne
- 1 bay leaf
  Salt and freshly ground black pepper
- 4–6 large eggs

FOR SERVING

- Crumbled feta cheese
- Chopped fresh herbs, such as dill, mint, and/or parsley
- Baguette, pita bread, or naan bread

SLOW COOKER JUMP STARTS
Up to 1 day ahead:
Cook the stovetop ingredients and refrigerate.
Combine the sauce ingredients (without the eggs) and refrigerate overnight.

RECIPE CONTINUES →

PREPARE THE STOVETOP INGREDIENTS

1 Heat the oil in a medium skillet over medium heat. Add the onion and garlic, and season with salt and pepper to taste. Cook, stirring, until the onion is softened, about 3 minutes. Add the tomato paste and cook, stirring, 30 to 60 seconds. (Alternatively, toss everything together in a heatproof bowl, and microwave on high, stirring once, until softened, 2 to 3 minutes.) Scrape the mixture into a 4- to 7-quart slow cooker.

ASSEMBLE THE SLOW COOKER

2 Add the tomatoes, roasted peppers, artichoke hearts, oil, cumin, sugar, paprika, cayenne, and bay leaf. Season with salt and pepper to taste and stir to combine. Cover and cook until the flavors have melded into a fragrant sauce, 4 to 6 hours on low or 2 to 3 hours on high.

3 Turn the slow cooker to high (if it's not on high already), and wait for the sauce to start bubbling slightly around the edges, 10 to 15 minutes. Season the sauce with salt and pepper to taste, then make four to six wells with a spoon (depending on how many eggs you're using) — the wells will be liquidy, but that's okay. Crack the eggs into the wells, and season them with salt and pepper to taste. Cover and cook until the whites are set but the yolks are still runny, 8 to 15 minutes.

SERVE

4 Scoop the stew and eggs into serving bowls, and sprinkle with feta and chopped fresh herbs. Serve with bread for mopping up the sauce.

STORAGE
The cooked shakshuka sauce without the eggs can be refrigerated for up to 5 days or frozen for up to 3 months. Reheat it in the slow cooker or on the stovetop before adding the eggs.

Slow-Cooked Applesauce

PREP TIME: 15 MINUTES

SLOW COOKER TIME: 4–5 HOURS ON LOW *or* 3–4 HOURS ON HIGH

MAKES
ABOUT 5 CUPS

When I discovered that I could make applesauce in the slow cooker, it was a total game changer. All I have to do is peel, core, and quarter apples; throw them into the slow cooker with a cinnamon stick, lemon juice, water, and a pinch of salt, and in a few hours, our house smells like heaven and we're left with the most beautiful applesauce imaginable. It's a great way to use up an apple-picking bounty or to get rid of slightly bruised or neglected fruit hanging out in the back of your crisper (you know they're there!). We eat the applesauce as is, or we serve it with yogurt and granola for a quick and nutritious breakfast (it's also delicious over French toast, pancakes, or waffles). Feel free to add other flavorings, such as a few thin slices of ginger, half a vanilla bean, or half a star anise pod.

SLOW COOKER

- 4 pounds sweet but crisp apples (such as Gala, Fuji, Honeycrisp, and/or Pink Lady), peeled, quartered, and cored (about 8 apples)
- ½ cup water
- 1 tablespoon lemon juice
- 1 cinnamon stick
  Pinch of salt

FOR SERVING

- Sugar, maple syrup, or honey (optional)
- Plain yogurt (optional)
- Granola (optional)

RECIPE CONTINUES →

ASSEMBLE THE SLOW COOKER

1 Combine the apples, water, lemon juice, cinnamon stick, and salt in a 4- to 7-quart slow cooker. Cover and cook, stirring once during cooking, until the apples are very soft, 4 to 5 hours on low or 3 to 4 hours on high.

FINISH AND SERVE

2 Remove and discard the cinnamon stick, and stir the sauce (the apples should be really soft and will break down naturally). You can leave it as is if you like a chunky texture, or you can purée it using an immersion blender for a smooth sauce. If the applesauce is tart (depending on the apples you used), feel free to sweeten it with sugar, maple syrup, or honey to taste.

3 Serve the applesauce as is, or turn it into breakfast by serving it with plain yogurt and a sprinkle of granola, if you'd like.

STORAGE
The applesauce can be refrigerated for up to 2 weeks or frozen for up to 3 months.

Peach Butter

PREP TIME: 20 MINUTES
SLOW COOKER TIME: 6–8 HOURS ON HIGH

MAKES
ABOUT 2¾ CUPS

This thick, rich peach butter is a cinch to make and enhances nearly any breakfast, from yogurt to waffles, pancakes, biscuits, and scones. I especially love spooning it on toast with fresh ricotta cheese — the creaminess of the ricotta is a heavenly match with the sweetness of the peaches. Speaking of heavenly matches, cardamom is hands down my favorite spice to pair with peaches, and here a couple of cardamom pods gently perfume the butter without overpowering the taste of the fruit (but they're optional). It's best to use ripe but firm peaches, which will be easier to peel (I use a vegetable peeler to do the job). And if breakfast isn't your thing, the peach butter is also awesome swirled into ice cream or layered into cookies or fruit bars!

SLOW COOKER

- 4 pounds peaches or nectarines, peeled, pitted, and coarsely chopped
- ⅔–¾ cup packed brown sugar
- 2 teaspoons lemon juice
- ¼ teaspoon fine sea salt
- 2 green cardamom pods (optional)

FOR SERVING

- Toasted bread (optional)
- Fresh ricotta cheese (optional)

ASSEMBLE THE SLOW COOKER

1 Combine the peaches, sugar to taste (according to the sweetness of your peaches), lemon juice, salt, and cardamom pods (if using) in a 4- to 7-quart slow cooker. Place a wooden spoon across the corner of the slow cooker, and set the lid on top so that it remains ajar (this will allow the steam to escape so that the butter can thicken). Cook on high, stirring occasionally, until the mixture is thick and syrupy, about 6 to 8 hours. Remove and discard the cardamom pods, and scrape the peaches into a blender; blend until smooth (or you can simply eat the warm peaches straight from the slow cooker!).

SERVE

2 Serve the peach butter warm or chilled.

STORAGE

The peach butter can be refrigerated for up to 3 weeks or frozen for up to 3 months.

Acknowledgments

First of all, thank you to my mom for convincing me to pull my dusty slow cooker out of the basement all those years ago. These recipes (and a zillion family meals!) wouldn't have happened without that nudging (and Dad, I'm not forgetting you — thanks for being a willing taste tester to these recipes!).

Thank you to my editor Deanna Cook, who saw the spark for this book well before I did. Your belief in me has helped shape my career, and I'm so grateful. Thanks also to Sarah Guare, Carolyn Eckert, Ash Austin, Deborah Balmuth, and the rest of the Storey team for supporting my vision and helping make the book the best it could be.

To the recipe testers who volunteered to cross-test these recipes, I'm beyond thankful for your time and input. Mary Kahn, Jessica Glasscoe, Tanya Rhodes, Sharron Hagge, Sharon Hagge

(there are two!), Ashley Strickland, Brady Montalbano, and Samantha Seneviratnae, you are all *amazing*.

Thank you to my incredible photography team for creating these beautiful images. Philip Flicks and Wei-Chia Huang, your skill is only matched by your kindness. Tehra Thorpe, you are a style queen (and can you reorganize my kitchen?). And thanks to Stephanie Stanczak, the ultimate sous chef, and Amy Kubik, our "set mom."

Finally, while being the husband/children of a food writer might sound fabulous, in reality it means you're often eating the same meals night after night (or in this case, slow cooked food for nine months straight). James, Ella, and Juni, thank you for not only being my biggest inspiration, but also for hanging in there with me throughout this journey. I love you beyond words.

Metric Conversion Charts

Unless you have finely calibrated measuring equipment, conversions between U.S. and metric measurements will be somewhat inexact. It's important to convert the measurements for all of the ingredients in a recipe to maintain the same proportions as the original.

VOLUME

TO CONVERT	TO	MULTIPLY
teaspoons	milliliters	teaspoons by 4.93
tablespoons	milliliters	tablespoons by 14.79
fluid ounces	milliliters	fluid ounces by 29.57
cups	milliliters	cups by 236.59
cups	liters	cups by 0.24
pints	milliliters	pints by 473.18
pints	liters	pints by 0.473
quarts	milliliters	quarts by 946.36
quarts	liters	quarts by 0.946

WEIGHT

TO CONVERT	TO	MULTIPLY
ounces	grams	ounces by 28.35
pounds	grams	pounds by 453.5
pounds	kilograms	pounds by 0.45

Index

Page numbers in *italic* indicate photos.

Stock Up on Kitchen Creativity
with More Books from Storey

ALSO FROM NICKI SIZEMORE

With this fuss-free formula you can create 77 delicious and nourishing grain bowls – from Sunshine Citrus and Coconut Cream to Curry-Roasted Salmon and Pork Bahn Mi Bowls – for any meal of the day. Countless customizing options help you suit individual diets and tastes.

BY RACHAEL NARINS

Make your skillet sizzle! These 40 recipes show off the versatility of this affordable and timeless cooking method, from cast-iron classics like cornbread, pan pizza, and the perfect grilled cheese sandwich to surefire favorites like Korean fried chicken, skillet catfish, and s'mores.

BY ELISABETH BAILEY

Transform your weeknight dinners with these 62 make-ahead, freezer-friendly sauces. Flavor-packed classics like All-American Barbecue and Sausage Ragu join creative combinations such as Chorizo Garlic, Pumpkin Coconut Cream, and Gorgonzola-Chive Butter, ensuring there's something for every taste.

BY OLWEN WOODIER

Liven up your cooking with an array of simple pestos, pastes, and purées that use just a few fresh ingredients and showcase flavors from around the globe. An additional 75 recipes encourage you to incorporate pestos into every meal.

Join the conversation. Share your experience with this book, learn more about Storey Publishing's authors, and read original essays and book excerpts at storey.com. Look for our books wherever quality books are sold or call 800-441-5700.